# SOLD
# AS IS

# SOLD AS IS

### ELLEN M. TRUE

**Outskirts Press, Inc.**
**Denver, Colorado**

The opinions expressed in this manuscript are solely the opinions of the author and do not represent the opinions or thoughts of the publisher. The author has represented and warranted full ownership and/or legal right to publish all the materials in this book.

Sold As Is
All Rights Reserved.
Copyright © 2011 Ellen M.True
soldasisbook@yahoo.com
v4.0 r1.1

This book may not be reproduced, transmitted, or stored in whole or in part by any means, including graphic, electronic, or mechanical without the express written consent of the publisher except in the case of brief quotations embodied in critical articles and reviews.

Outskirts Press, Inc.
http://www.outskirtspress.com

ISBN: 978-1-4327-6096-0

Outskirts Press and the "OP" logo are trademarks belonging to Outskirts Press, Inc.

PRINTED IN THE UNITED STATES OF AMERICA

# Dedication

This book is dedicated to the following people, each of whom, in their own way, served as members of the crew on this journey (even when it seemed like it might end up like the Titanic!)

This is a quote that I thought of often during my renovating experience,
*"Waves are not measured in feet or inches,
they are measured in increments of fear."*
Buzzy Trent—A Pioneer of big wave surfing.

A special thanks to Nathan Dougherty, my editor who provided me with direction and proofreading.
The beautiful illustrations were drawn by Evie Douglas.
My appreciation goes out to my parents who had the faith that I would succeed.

# SOLD AS IS

To Julie my niece who encouraged me to unlatch the door of my creativity, and I saw the world.

A big thank you goes to Glenn and Amy for sharing your riveting stories and construction advice.

To my dream designer team of Marti and Bob who helped to keep me on the construction path.

To Linda and Ken, thank you for joining my voyage and holding on with me through swells and daily tides.

Debbie and Mick, your support was soaked up like a sponge, there was no tree too high or stump too big that you couldn't tackle.

Amy and Michael, you flowed with optimism and helped to steer me in the right direction (EAST).

Ann Margaret, I am indebted to you for your book review and your advice on how to act like an author.

Matt, Charmaine, Aubrey, and Teagan, if there's a good neighbor hall of fame you all deserve to be in it.

John and Marion, God works in mysterious ways and we are living examples of his humor.

When the thunder storms raged Sharon and Ted were the light house keepers flashing the ray of hope.

And to all my future sailors—Max, Jack, Josef, Maria, Tommy, Tony, Michael, Ali, Tucker, Taryn, Trenton, Emma and Miguel.

# Prologue

In the spring of 2008 I purchased my father's cottage on Conesus Lake, near Rochester N.Y. This story is about my experience of turmoil and fulfillment while renovating an 85 year old summer cottage with strong ties to family now and a century ago. Intertwined are family adventures and Lake lore stories about having a summer cottage on the water over the generations.

It is about valuing the past while forging ceaselessly forward to the future as I experienced my own personal growth. I hope it inspires people to follow their dreams and to accept mistakes as a learning opportunity to change direction. I want to be a role model for those who don't want to be held back by lack of funds or knowledge. An inspiration for others to follow their passion when only fear is holding them back, where success is measured when you have followed with your heart.

# Table of Contents

The Green Light..................................................................1
Follow my Compass .........................................................5
"Sold As Is"......................................................................11
Just Another Day.............................................................17
Lake Lore: Through the Generations.............................21
Lake Lore: Treasure Hunt...............................................27
Lake Lore: Mystical Snipe Hunt ....................................29
Lake Lore: Swim Across the Lake .................................33
Lake Lore: Tunnel under the Lake ................................39
Contractor Blues .............................................................47
Design the New Cottage.................................................53
Meet the Code Officer ...................................................57
Laying the Foundation of Change .................................63
Lake Lore: Brown Station Wagon .................................73
Lake Lore: Waterskiing...................................................77
Lake Lore: Crash Goes Grandma...................................81

Lake Lore: Snowmobiles on Thin Ice ..................89
Lake Lore: Scuba Diving—
    Unexpected Complications ...........................................97
Unleashing my Power of Creativity ............................... 107
Shattered Dreams .............................................................. 117
Rental Woes ........................................................................ 125
Flying Unwelcome Guests May 2008 ........................... 135
Revenge of the Bees .......................................................... 145
Lake Lore: Explosion on the 3rd of July ...................... 151
Lake Lore: Mutiny on the Water July 2005 .................. 155
The Keys to my Success ................................................... 165
Healing Waters ................................................................... 177
What's Next ........................................................................ 195

# The Green Light

One fall morning as the sun was peeking into the cold sky, I jogged down the sidewalk near my house in Henrietta, N.Y., a suburb of Rochester. I felt empty inside, but I couldn't figure out where it came from—I was content in my life, with a good job, nice house and many relationships. It had been lingering for months, maybe years, but this day it was especially strong. After some soul searching, I realized that some force was pulling me away from my unfulfilled suburban life. It was directing me somewhere familiar, a place I had always felt in harmony with life. I needed to live on the water. I slowed down to a walk as I entered a wooded trail off the road and reflected upon my situation. I began to feel more clarity to sort out my complex feelings. About an hour later I emerged, feeling content that I had found my answers

The natural solution would be to purchase my father's

## SOLD AS IS

cottage on Conesus Lake, about 20 miles from my home, but he never expressed any interest in selling it. It had been in our family for decades and there was no concrete plan of how ownership would be split among my five older siblings. The cottage could also only be used six months out of the year and the only water source came from the lake. Before I could live there year round it would need major renovations, a challenge for me because I didn't have any construction experience.

With those obstacles looming heavy in my path, I hired a real estate agent that same afternoon and began seeking out other lakefront properties that were already year round. Weeks went by and I noticed that none of the other cottages felt right. The other places were just normal, the family cottage was special. I realized that it was the history and family connection that I wanted. My father's cottage was the piece of my puzzle I needed to fulfill my desire and the timing was right. He was approaching 80 years old and needed to plan for how the cottage would be preserved for the future.

I was concerned about the financial burden such an undertaking would place on me. I am a manager in a hospital performing EEG's (brainwaves) and sleep studies. Lakefront property is expensive to purchase and maintain, and if I really wanted to live there I would need to sell my house.

While sitting at the crossroads of my life, the light turned green. After I explained to my dad my desire to

## THE GREEN LIGHT

live at the lake and my plans for the cottage, he agreed to sell it to me. I made a difficult decision, but I shifted into high gear and crashed through my roadblocks of doubt, fear and excuses. I was embarking on an adventure of a lifetime that would change my world as I followed my passion.

# Follow my Compass

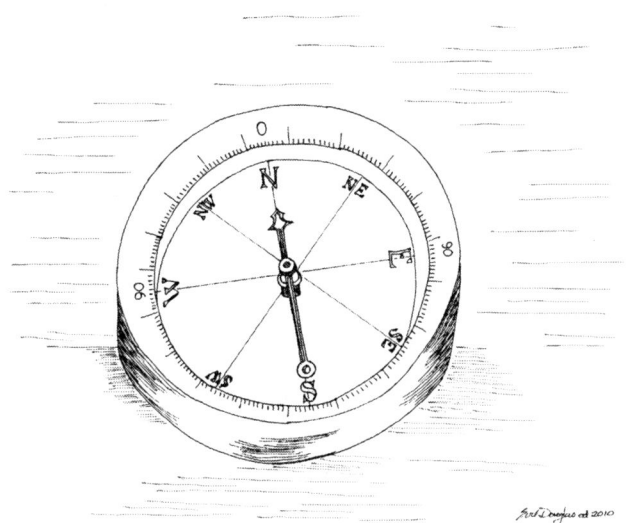

Before I could purchase the cottage I had to clear the hurdle of trying to sell my three-bedroom ranch house. I needed the equity as a down payment for the renovations.

It was February 16, and a wave of accomplishment washed over me. This was the day I had planned to put the house up for sale, the culmination of weeks of preparation to sort out, tediously clean and move out furniture.

# SOLD AS IS

I had enthusiasm as I anticipated starting the next chapter in my life.

Clouds can foretell coming events, and in the days leading up to the scheduled listing they were dense and dark. A heavy rain fell for days with gray encompassing the sky. The water pooled outside on the lawn before it drained into the basement, causing it to flood. I was in utter disbelief about the timing of the wet basement as I sloshed around in a foot of ice cold water. I shivered and attempted to stay dry while I unhooked the broken sump pump. My stomach churned, I rubbed my tired eyes and started to sob.

Jay and his wife Lisa, my real estate agents and also my friends, offered reassurance. It was clear that the house would not possess a "For Sale" on the front lawn that day. Jay and Lisa stood at the top of the basement stairs, looking down to see me standing in the middle of the muddy water. My face was puffy and my nose sniffled in a feeble attempt to hold back the tears.

"It will be okay, this is just a setback," Lisa said.

Water dripped off my clothes as I tromped up the stairs. I plopped on the couch with a towel draped around my neck. Jay shifted his weight as he looked me in the eye with a genuine smile.

"The economy is on a serious downswing," he said. "There's an over-abundance of houses on the market. Ellen, you have to set yourself apart from other sellers if you want to sell, let alone get full value. First, hire an

## FOLLOW MY COMPASS

excavation company to dry your basement. Then paint every room, including the ceilings, and replace the carpets. Finally, the roof is marginal and will exclude some buyers. You have to put on a new one."

I was dumbfounded by his bluntness, but I trusted Jay and knew he was trying to set me up for success. I just had a hard time dealing with the wave of disappointment that washed over me. I stared at the floor unable to make eye contact. My eyes filled with water and I swallowed hard as tears trickled down. His words echoed loudly in my mind: You will have to spend thousands of dollars and your dream will be on hold.

They left as I slouched low on the couch by myself. The flooded basement opened a Pandora's Box of projects that would need to be completed. It was only 10 a.m. but felt like midnight to my emotionally exhausted body. My pity party lasted 30 minutes until I made myself snap back. I understood that I needed to let the intrusive thoughts pass through without taking up space in my mind. The negative chatter became quiet, the stagnation and doubt left my mind and I grabbed a ballpoint pen to develop a plan. I could choose how to feel, and I would not allow myself to be a victim of these circumstances. In order to succeed I needed to feel rejuvenated and realigned, so I had to shift my thoughts toward being empowered.

My intention was to have Jay's to-do list completed in less than a month, with a targeted listing date of March 15. I started to schedule days off from work and recruited

## SOLD AS IS

help from my friends, determined to get the most for my time and money. It took me three weeks to paint every wall, molding and ceiling then put up new kitchen wallpaper. I interviewed four roofing companies, but their best estimates were all to expensive for my tight budget. A friend recommended a roofing contractor who was able to start right away and because the cold February temperatures had slowed up the roofing business I was able to negotiate a better price. I hired a handyman to re-hang my gutters to divert the water away from the slope of the house but decided not to hire an excavator to complete the foundation drainage work because it would take too long and cost too much. Instead I would just note the moisture in the basement on my property disclosure form.

The sound of the hammer was joy to my ears a few weeks later when the red, and white and blue Re/Max realtor's "For Sale" sign was pounded into the lawn. I felt relief and pride passing another milestone toward my passion. The house was listed on the real estate market at 9 a.m. of my target date. Four hours later Jay called to say he showed it to one couple and already received an offer. He wanted us to review it as soon as possible but warned me that first offers are traditionally low.

I drove to his house brimming with optimism. I sang out loud with the car stereo, swaying back and forth and hoping no one would judge my vocal performance. I just couldn't believe I had gotten an offer so soon. The door at Jay and Lisa's house opened a crack and Max, their

## FOLLOW MY COMPASS

redheaded five-year-old, peaked out. We walked hand-in-hand to the dining room where Jay had been waiting anxiously for my arrival. The tone of the room changed when I saw him sitting rigid with a dull expression. The contract was laid face down in front of him, his hands neatly folded with fingers interlaced to protect the information. Jay looked serious as he shuffled the papers back and forth.

"First of all, you don't have to take the first offer," he said matter-of-factly. "They didn't give us the asking price."

He grasped one form and slowly turned it face up, sliding it across the oak table like a dealer at a poker game. He smiled at me and waited.

My eyes darted back and forth as I read the document. My mouth dropped open and I gasped as I saw their offer, $200 over the listed price. The buyer had cash and requested a closing date of less than a month.

Jay winked and his hardened poker face melted. Smiling, he went on to explain that the buyers immediately fell in love with my house. They were aware of other viewings scheduled that afternoon and offered over the listed price hoping I would accept their bid and pull it off the market. They didn't even care about the wet basement. It was the best situation I could have asked for. Even with the odds of stiff competition and a poor economy stacked against me, the house sold only in four hours. To me that was something just short of a

## SOLD AS IS

miracle. Contagious smiles and giggles flowed out as we slapped high fives all around the room.

I realized that when things were meant to be they would flow easily, that doors would open just when obstacles appeared to block the way. For the first time since deciding to buy the cottage I felt like my internal compass was pointed in the right direction. Now I was floating downstream, not fighting the current as I had been living at my house in the suburbs.

# "Sold As Is"

My mind raced, my attention span struggling to hold a thought for more than a few seconds. Closing day was the culmination of a lengthy and arduous process to purchase my father's cottage. It was the official start of a new chapter in my life, a new reality. I felt tingly inside. I was about to accomplish my dream.

But still some sadness gnawed at me. For my father it was the final transfer of the beloved lakefront property that was a significant part his life. He had taken a leap of faith that I would be able to transform the cottage, even with so many factors stacked against me.

I met my parents Ruth and Blair at the large Victorian house that served as the office for our lawyer Nancy at 10 a.m. sharp. It was cold for May at 50 degrees and I wasn't dressed warm enough, shivering as I walked briskly along with my parents. My father stepped tentatively up onto the

# SOLD AS IS

wooden porch, stopping a moment to catch his breath.

Nancy smiled as she greeted us, then ushered us to sit down at the large wooden table. She took her position at the head of the table while I sat across from my parents, the table acting as a barrier between us. I leaned on the table and rubbed my eyes as Nancy pulled out a folder with a very official looking stack of papers.

"This will be very straightforward," she said with confidence. "It should not take long."

She eased through form after form, pointing to where we had to initial the bottom of the page and explaining each line in detail. One set listed the contents of the cottage that would be sold with the structure—the docks, life jackets and even the antique duck decoys.

Nancy shuffled deeper into the pile of papers and pulled out a real estate disclosure form.

"This document requires the sellers to disclose any mechanical or structural deficits known on the property."

She hesitated a moment, then continued.

"Let's review this in great detail."

She laid down her paper and turned to look at my parents.

"When was the last time the chimney was cleaned?"

"I can't ever remember that it was ever cleaned," my mother answered sheepishly. "Blair, do you remember?"

"No," he said. "It has not been cleaned."

Nancy started to check the little boxes that showed the good faith answers, and then turned to my parents again.

# "SOLD AS IS"

"Due to its age the house must be tested for lead paint. Does it have any interior lead paint that you know of?" Nancy's eyes grew wide as she looked at my mother. "Has the house been tested for lead paint?"

"No," they answered together.

"It has not been tested for lead paint," Dad said with confidence. "The cottage does not have any paint at all inside."

"The basement is a place where moisture problems can arise," Nancy continued. "Is there any moisture or water in the basement?"

"No, there is no moisture," my father answered quickly "The cottage rests on top of cement pillars. Good thing there was no basement when we had a flood decades ago. The lake water rose right up to the bottom of the cottage."

"How about smoke and carbon monoxide detectors? How many are on the premises?"

"None," my mother answered.

Slightly concerned, Nancy looked up and stretched her neck forward. She told my parents that by law they were required to get some installed. My mother hesitated, and then made eye contact for me to lean forward. After seconds of awkwardness, I leaned in to her.

"Make sure you buy some smoke detectors," she whispered.

Nancy too looked like she had something to say, but instead was silent for a moment. She examined the bottom

## SOLD AS IS

of the paper, and then slowly looked up.

"Have you ever seen any termites or other insects? Or has an insect inspection been performed?"

"Yes, we had termites once, about 20 years ago," my father answered. "The exterminator took care of the infestation. I am sure it is okay now. We have not seen any evidence of them since then."

Nancy turned to me. "Who did you have for a home inspection, Ellen?"

Before I could open my mouth to respond, Dad spoke up.

"There was not one. With the condition of the cottage it would not have passed any house inspection."

Nancy looked astonished and countered to me jokingly, "Are you sure you know what you are getting into?" I replied with a laugh and a bashful smile.

I put my hand on my forehead, rubbed my eyes and yawned. I had become weary of all the questions and the same answers over and over again. I started to wonder whether I was crazy to want to buy this cottage, which was starting to sound more like a money pit. It probably did look that way to Nancy, but I knew it was the right thing to do and so did my parents. I could see my parents growing weary of the process too as they shifted their weight in the wooden chairs. Dad's eyes glazed over, I sensed his impatience as he rubbed his temples with two fingers. Suddenly he leaned closer to see the lawyer.

"Do we, really have to finish this form?" he whispered

## "SOLD AS IS"

to Nancy, a bit of hesitancy in his voice. "This has become a lengthy, tedious process. Can't you just write across the contract "Sold As Is" in large letters instead of having to list all the numerous deficits?"

Nancy searched for an answer, peered down at the form and with an eyebrow cocked, shrugged her shoulders. In a peppy voice she said, "Sure I can do that," and wrote Sold As Is.

Despite all the problems I understood what I had bought. I realized it would be an uphill struggle at times to fix it all but worth the reward. It wasn't just some sagging neglected cottage, it was my dream house by the water. I remembered a quote by Christopher Reeve, *"Either you decide to stay in the shallow end of the pool or go out in the ocean."* I was ready to swim deep in my new ocean. Cottage construction would be filled with rip tides, sharks and storms but also provide brilliant sunsets, calm days and serenity. "Sold As Is" was what my new life was all about.

# Just Another Day

What is the cottage like in the lazy summer days? I can recollect a recent day that, for me, epitomizes life on the lake. I have visions of a kaleidoscope of towels hung in array over the porch rail as the kids searched for their favorite one. Shivering children running inside, the screen door slamming as their stomachs growled and lake water dripped from their bathing suits. Directed to no one special their high pitched voices said, "What can we eat?"

The sun and the clouds had played a game of peek a boo with the children. They ran around and giggled as the hundreds of tiny bubbles they created drifted around the lawn, just to pop when then landed.

At the lake I enjoy the simple pleasure of sitting on the porch in the antique rocking chairs under the slowly turning ceiling fans. As I sat on this day, attempting to solve the world's problems, the next door neighbor stopped by

## SOLD AS IS

and picked up a glass of lemonade while sitting in the wicker chair. The porch is surrounded by colorful flowers flowing over the edge of the flower boxes.

The seagulls spotted bread that floated, swooping down while they fought each other in mid air. One gull fell out of the light blue sky as it gained balance and dipped into the water, skimming off with a piece of bread in his beak. The commotion was heard from the kids who held their hands over their heads as they laughed while the adults shooed away the birds.

I walked out to the water to see the younger kids jumping off the dock one by one. As they swim by their little heads bobbed to the surface, spitting and sputtering the water while they rubbed their eyes.

"Let's do it again," they shrieked, and then swam back with smiles and determination.

At the dock passengers lined up to go waterskiing. I stepped carefully onto the pontoon boat and felt the anticipation growing while I balanced music, drinks and suntan lotion in my arms for the ride we were about to take. I lounged back and smiled as the boat pulled away from the hoist. I felt the breeze and tried to try to find some sun beneath the puffy clouds. When the sun finally did reach me the warming rays brought relief from the slight chill in the air. The others on the boat relaxed comfortably while they picked out the beautiful lake houses they wished they owned.

My friends on the shore laughed and smiled while they

## JUST ANOTHER DAY

sat in the Adirondack chairs. They pointed to the unique boats they saw and said hello to the kayakers who paddled by effortlessly. The sunbathers caught up on the latest gossip in the slick new magazines.

On the lake, the WaveRunners left a trail of white water spraying behind them, and just beyond them a small sailboat sat motionless. Eventually it had to be towed in after the inexperienced captain vowed it wasn't her fault but the strong wind. She was red-faced in embarrassment and wondered where all the people came from as they clapped and cheered while she sat smiling as she held the broken tiller.

This is a routine day at the cottage on Conesus Lake.

# Lake Lore: Through the Generations

The cottage had been part of my family for generations and as long as we owned it we journaled what life was like there. As I pulled open a drawer a month after I moved in I came across a photo album that contained vintage photographs, receipts and postcards my ancestors had used to chronicle decades of trials and triumphs at the lake. The individual pictures were unceremoniously tacked down on stock paper. I was amazed that the frail artifacts had survived over a century of wear and tear. With my paper treasures suspended in time, I embarked on a journey to discover the lives of my ancestors during the lake's heyday around the turn of the century.

The black and white scenes depicted a time of amazing growth and change for America, bringing to life a world I only knew from history books. Theodore Roosevelt was

## SOLD AS IS

the 26th president of the United States. Albert Einstein had just published papers that introduced the theory of relativity. The Wright brothers' airplane stayed airborne for 39 minutes, the longest flight ever.

The pictures revealed fashion that was grand, both formal and romantic. Women wore ornate dresses corseted to a small waist with larger-than-life hats. The men wore suspenders, derby hats and long slim trousers. In a world void of phonographs, movies, radio and television, the evenings were filled with family gatherings around the piano or sing-a-longs with a hand-cranked Victrola.

During the early 1900s postcards were the main source of communication and most economical, costing only a penny to mail. From the letters I learned that my great grandfather George purchased the lake property in 1903, he became one of the 200 original property owners that called Conesus Lake their own. He built a two-story cottage nestled under the canopy of mature Cottonwood trees near the water's edge.

The structure—like most of its era—was heated with a coal stove and lit with kerosene lamps. House fires were a common occurrence. Without any established roads or electricity around the lake it was difficult to suppress a fire when it started, and it appears the cottage suffered this fate. The original cottage most likely burned down as it was replaced with another cottage just two decades later.

George's preferred mode of travel to Conesus Lake in the warm summer of 1903 was the horse and buggy. With

# THROUGH THE GENERATIONS

only 8,000 cars and 10 miles of paved roads in the whole United States, automobiles were still a novelty. Buying a new car would have been unreachable for George, as the average price of a Ford listed at $900. Before he retired as a dairy farmer, George made $12.98 per week for 59 hours work.

It was essential that they planned carefully because it took them at least five hours to travel the 37 miles by buggy. Things didn't get any easier after they set out, especially for the horses. It was common for the one-lane dirt road to be washed out or scattered with stray rocks. George and his family had to stop halfway through the journey at a special Hickory tree so his Standardbred horse could rest and drink from a nearby stream. The faded pictures show George standing on the dock while his horses swam in the water after the long trek to the lake.

The postcards from 1905 reflect a more efficient way to travel to the cottage than the horse and buggy. It was the locomotive. The train started in Rochester 28 miles away and zig-zagged through little towns, ending near the pier where the passengers would exit to board large boats. The excursion locomotive provided a connection for the steamboats that transported passengers to their destinations around the waterway.

The image of dark smoke billowing from the chimney stacks of the majestic McPherson Steamboat was on numerous postcards. The McPherson was the largest of the excursion boats at 120 feet and had triple decks that easily

## SOLD AS IS

held up to 1,000 passengers and old time bands playing for hours as entertainment. The vessels were essential for mail and grocery delivery because the road around the lake would not be completed for another 25 years.

As I sifted through the album one picture called out to me. It displayed a five-foot high crescent wooden sign that read "Cedar Crest" which they posted high above the end of the dock. My ancestors waited under the sign in anticipation of the small steamer boat. The weathered sign had been passed down through many generations and still hangs proudly on the boat shed today.

I put the pictures away and walked outside and gazed up at the cottage. The land beneath my feet and the wooden structure represented thousands of memories created over the generations. Some are lost to time, but many others will live on in our hearts and the faded pictures tacked to the stock paper. I wonder what my ancestors would think of me, a free-spirited, independent woman who renovated their cottage, one that now has electricity, plumbing and a furnace.

Now that I am a permanent part of the history of Cedar Crest cottage I feel very humbled and honored to pass the cottage on to the next generation. I continue the tradition of sending postcards to family and friends as I enjoy sharing my adventures. And I will add my pictures to the collection so future generations will know what it was like living on the lake in this 21st century.

My ancestors waiting for a steamboat ride in 1905.

The Cedar Crest sign is mounted on the boat shed in this century.

All dressed up for swim in front of cottage in 1903.

The steam boats catered to a thriving tourist business in 1910.

The grocery and mail was delivered around the cottages and camps.

A glimpse of touring in style at the lakes heyday during the turn of the century.

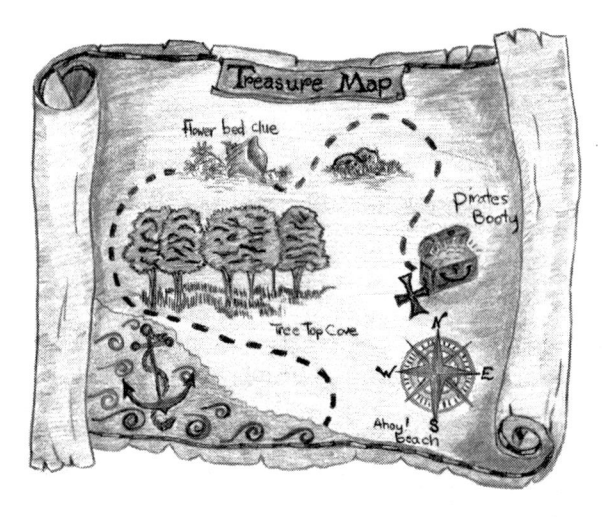

# Lake Lore: Treasure Hunt

Friends and family have enjoyed the wonder of the cottage, but it has always been especially fun for the children who came. They experience the joy of playing near the water, whether it was a treasure hunt for the pirate's booty or collecting sea shells.

One mid-summer day the kids wanted to search for

## SOLD AS IS

hidden treasure, or "pirate's booty" as they called it. I told the kids I would hide a treasure box and whoever finds it can have all the "jewels" inside. They stood at the shore and anxiously counted to 100 while I hid the wooden box. It resembled a small brown treasure chest with a wooden round top and dark leather straps.

The game had begun. They held tightly the worn pirate map I had made for them, the adventure seekers looking for the black X that marked the spot. They looked at the ground as they searched under the sailboats and kayaks. The map led them to a conch shell that was placed in the flower bed, and inside was another clue that said the booty was "high as tree tops." One of the boys started to look up in the trees but Jack, the oldest of the pirates at seven, had another idea and led the group into the house. He went up the stairs to get to a higher level, the same as tree tops. There they scoured under beds and below dressers.

"I have the pirate's booty," Jack called out. He started laughing as he mimicked a pirate. "Aunt Ellen you promised we could have the treasure inside, right?"

I remembered that the box contained a match box sports car; I had inadvertently forgotten that I had left $200 in the box to pay a contractor. The kids bolted down the stairs waving handfuls of twenty dollar bills.

Now it was my turn to play pirate and steal back my money. We played hide and go seek as I pried the stolen cash from their little hands. We all laughed and smiled.

"Can we play again?" Jack asked

# Lake Lore:
# Mystical Snipe Hunt

---

*"Perhaps no one dreamed of a snipe an hour ago, but as soon as the dusk begins you hear this peculiar spirit-suggesting sound, now heard through and above the evening dim sounds of the village."*

Henry David Thoreau—American author

Near the shore strange sounds radiated back toward the cottage—a loud cluck, cluck then a long, high pitched whistle. I immediately recognized the sounds of the annual snipe hunt and started to chuckle.

The tall tale began a few hours earlier. Five-year old Josef had asked his father's friend John for an empty mayonnaise jar so he and his brother Jack could catch fireflies. But John had other ideas for the boys.

## SOLD AS IS

My cousin John was a tall slender man with a constant warm smile. He always looked forward to having new visitors to the cottage, especially ones he could talk into a snipe hunt. The twinkle in his eye was evident as he bent down to the boys' level.

"Have you ever been here at the cottage before?" he asked.

Quinn, Jack and Josef's best friend, shook his head no.

"Have you ever snipe hunted?"

Quinn looked skeptical, not sure he understood what John had just asked. John was in full swing, ready to tell the tales about the fictitious snipe. The three boys listened, wide eyed and silent.

"Are we allowed to hunt snipe?" Jack asked.

"We all can snipe hunt," my Dad chimed in, and then flashed a big mischievous smile.

"Really? What does it look like?" Josef looked puzzled.

My Dad and John motioned the curious children toward the edge of the water. John's description of the snipe was vague. It was a wild animal that looked like a quail with yellow brown feathers, a short black neck and a long flat beak. It was not too tall, but not too short. When it was hungry it clucked like a chicken. He explained that snipe are commonly found in marshy shorelines, just like at the lake. Josef now grew very curious and paid close attention to the details.

## MYSTICAL SNIPE HUNT

"How do you catch a snipe?" he asked.

John explained in a matter of fact tone that the hunter doesn't use a gun but a burlap bag. He reached in to his back pocket and pulled out a small booklet titled "The Official Boy Scout Snipe Manual."

"The snipe hunt should occur just before sundown," he read. "You must make sure the light is just right. If it is too early in the evening the snipe might see the hunters. If it is too late the snipe would have already eaten and be too full."

John said the more kids involved in the snipe hunt the better the chance at bagging a snipe, so he asked the kids to go and recruit other young hunters. The group quickly grew to five kids, all excited to start the adventure.

John lined up the kids and handed out the supplies. Because this was his first snipe hunt and he was the most enthusiastic, Quinn was elected to hold the most important position. John grabbed the brown bag and rolled down the edges while he gave specific instructions: The mouth had to be held open at least 12 inches while the bottom was dragged along the ground. The rest of the curious helpers carried the other tools, including a silver flashlight and a yellow snipe whistle.

"I was lucky tonight to be able to locate the special whistle to help attract the snipe," John said. "But you could also use two long sticks to bang against each other."

"The flashlight attracts the snipe," he continued. "They are hypnotized by the flicker and will come just like

# SOLD AS IS

insects to a bug zapper. As soon as he notices the beam of light the snipe will scurry into the open sack." John showed Quinn how to close the bag quickly and seal it tight to capture a fast-moving snipe.

The dwindling daylight hours flowed into the glowing sunset, and the conditions were perfect. All along the property the children scoured for the elusive bird, walking slowly while they made loud clucking sounds. Quinn listened intently as Josef blew the special whistle, waited a few seconds then clucked a few more times. One by one the seasoned hunters sneaked back to the cottage while Quinn examined the roots under the cottonwood tree. After about a minute he looked up and realized he was alone.

On the porch loud giggles replaced the snipe calls. Jack spilled the beans and told Quinn that snipe is a made-up bird and he was the star of the hopeless chase. The kids didn't want Quinn to feel singled out so they retold the stories of when they first held the burlap bag. Quinn was reassured that he was part of a unique club of hunters and could join the other side of the snipe hunts that would continue over the generations whenever someone new visited the cottage.

# Lake Lore:
# Swim Across the Lake

*"You can't put a limit on anything.
The more you dream, the farther you get."*
Michael Phelps—Eight time Olympic gold medalist

The date on the calendar was circled in red—July 29, the annual swim across the lake day. It was about one mile across but the way the swimmers told it the distance was roughly as long as the English Channel. The eight swimmers were jubilant as they arrived early in the afternoon. They had bragged to their friends and family about the great athletic feat they were about to attempt and the conditions couldn't have been better. The large cirrus clouds had drifted away and the day was filled with rays

## SOLD AS IS

of sun that cut the slight coolness in the air.

The event would be divided between two groups, the wannabe athletes and a five-person boat crew. Their 22-foot pontoon boat had a flat bottom supported by two metal cylinders, similar to a houseboat. The boat crew would follow along, protecting us from other boats and unseen harm. Their responsibility was to coach the swimmers and become a lifeguard if a fatigued swimmer needed assistance. They also had an array of food like warm baked brownies, snacks, junk food and were stocked with other critical items like tropical music, suntan lotion, cameras and gossip magazines.

The eager group of athletes gathered at the shore as I gave a pep talk about the lake temperature, wind speed and the importance of hydration. I also clarified the rules of the swim. We had to travel in a pack; "Never swim alone" was my motto. We would not permit wet suits, life jackets or any device that floated as these gave an unfair advantage. We would all begin at the same time, but setbacks would be expected. If someone couldn't complete the swim it was okay for them stop. They would signal the boat and ride back, but could be subjected to the ridicule of the boat crew. I looked to the other side of the lake and determined that to swim a straight course we needed a constant reference point, so we chose the enormous brown house directly across from the cottage.

We pressed up against the cottonwood tree and stretched our biceps, triceps and calf muscles. We talked

## SWIM ACROSS THE LAKE

like professional athletes and compared swim styles such as the freestyle, backstroke, breast stroke, butterfly and even the doggy paddle. Realistically most of us would just improvise. When we put on our goggles, a kaleidoscope of different colors, it signaled official start of the swim. We didn't have to worry about what order to start as there was no Olympic qualifying trial for our event. Our methods to enter the water varied from the cannonball off the dock to wading in from shore.

Once in the water I felt energized. My feet recoiled as the slimy seaweed tickled the bottoms and gradually I became more horizontal. When I reached full speed I skimmed the surface like a water bug. As the water got deeper, my mind wondered about the vast depths beneath me, the animals with rows of razor-sharp teeth that would love to take a bite out of a swimmer. Instead I focused my thoughts on matching my rhythmic pattern of my stroke with deep breaths.

More than halfway into our endeavor it became clear there was no turning back. I listened to chatter from other swimmers about fatigue and giving up, but I knew my biggest obstacle was my mind, not my body. Doubts started to bubble to the surface from my unconscious mind. They told me it was too far to swim, that I wanted to quit, but I refused to validate these psychological barriers. I looked up to see the other heads bobbing above the water in a steady, synchronized rhythm. My pattern was geared toward efficiency to give me a competitive

## SOLD AS IS

edge—breathe deeply, breast stroke, crawl, breast stroke, breathe. I gained momentum by bending and kicking my legs just like a frog. If I looked up to check the destination point it would break the rhythm of my stroke, and I knew I could get off course quickly if I didn't keep my full attention on the pattern.

Behind me I heard a swimmer call for the boat. He swam to the back as the engine was shut off, then grasped the ladder and held it gingerly as he boarded to safety. The boat crew was compassionate and offered high calorie food to help alleviate the fallen swimmer's disappointment.

We were only 100 feet from the dock, so I offered fragmented phrases in an attempt to motivate the other swimmers to the finish line.

"Sharks sink if they stop swimming. Don't be a shark."

"Help, help. Oh, it hurts," I heard someone shouting.

On the boat they cut the motor and the music to hear better and the cries became louder. The people in the boat turned to look at the commotion and saw that the gasps spewed from my friend Mike. He abruptly halted his swim and contorted his panic-stricken face. Mike thrashed in the water, unable to articulate his situation. My mind ran wild as I wondered, was it a fish that bit him or was he injured somehow? In broken sentences he said he had a leg cramp and his calf muscle was fully contracted. Mike continued to flail through the water to the dock in front of him. He flopped down on the dock and writhed in

## SWIM ACROSS THE LAKE

pain, unable to speak at first. Slowly he stretched and the intense sensation subsided. He had a soaked ego, but he had finished the swim even as he limped across the finish line. We shared in triumph as we waded back in the shallow water. I stood with goose bumps and shivered. The swim invigorated our bodies as it warmed our souls.

∽∾

Once I was back in cottage, other friends called and said, "Did we miss the annual swim across the lake?" I didn't have the heart to tell them they had.

"Let's do it tomorrow," I said. And we did.

# Lake Lore: Tunnel under the Lake

Practical jokes are part of the cottage life, and over the generations these stories are carried on and passed along. It was mid August 2009. The cottage was stuffy, the lake still—the kind of a day only a swimmer could enjoy. I paddled my yellow kayak close to the shore a mile down the lake to my friends Bob and Marti's house.

Savoring the half hour paddle ride, I peered around and looked at the orange lilies lining the water's edge. A dragonfly landed on the hull, almost hypnotized. I felt the stress of the day melt off of me like an ice cream cone dripping in the heat. I dropped my hand into the water to cool off and let it trail behind me as it created rows of ripples. I looked down into the water and noticed the seaweed that proliferated the shallow areas waving with the current. I arrived and nudged the kayak past their

## SOLD AS IS

wooden dock, then heaved the small boat out of the water. I looked forward to cheerful conversation, the scent of the barbecue beef drawing me in.

Bob and Marti, both retired, had married just a few years earlier. They have a synchronicity about them, frequently finishing each other's sentences. We sat outside on the porch and watched the evening darkness slowly encroach the daylight. I laughed and pointed when I spotted a checkered black and white loon. We watched as it ungracefully took off, swimming first until the wind helped him gain enough speed to take off.

I relived a story when a bunch of kids were at the cottage eager to learn about lake animals. I told them about the invisible loon who will dive underwater, resurface a safe distance away and then dive again. I described the solitary loon call like a yodel or a laugh or even a wail, and then we practiced it together. With my remote hidden in my hand, I played actual loon calls on the stereo for the fascinated kids. At times it sounded like a whole flock was close at the dock. I stared out the window, with big eyes and a surprised facial expression. I pointed and pretended to be amazed by the number of birds. The young children also heard the familiar sounds and ran past me to the water, but quickly realized they were unable to find the elusive birds. I reminded them that the birds can stay submerged for a long time until they feel safe to surface. They scanned the water for any motion, but became confused when the loon calls continued without any sight of

# TUNNEL UNDER THE LAKE

the birds. They traced the yodel sounds only to discover they came from the stereo speaker. With my red face and slight smile, I had to fess up and we all laughed together as they vowed to get even with me.

Bob laughed and said, "That wasn't very nice of you to play a practical joke on the little kids."

Then he smiled and turned toward me. "Your family has owned the cottage for years, you must have heard about the Conesus Lake tunnel?"

"What tunnel," I said right on cue with a lift of my eyebrows.

"Holmes Hill Road is perpendicular to, and ends at the lake. There are no houses or cottages built there," Bob said with a change of inflection to show he was serious. "Directly across the lake on the other side is another road. It looks just like you could drive down the road and go under the lake to get the other side."

Bob was right, I thought. I had driven down the road previously and it looked just like he described. My jaw dropped open. I clung to his every word. I never heard anything about this before and I was desperate to learn more.

In a flat tone he stated, "During World War II, the government decided it was critically important to build a tunnel under the lake to move important military supplies. It was built by the prisoners and out-of-work tradesmen and took about a year to complete. The distance was a little less than a mile across. This tunnel was a way that

## SOLD AS IS

the military saved time. They would be able to get from one side to the other in half the time it would take them to drive all around the lake. And in the event of a national emergency, civilian cars would be allowed to travel through the tunnel."

I sat on the edge of my seat, propping myself up on my elbows. I listened intently as Bob went into great detail.

"The tunnel was musty with curled paint chips that clung to the walls, and steady droplets of water seeping through the tiny cracks from the lake above. A row of lights hung all along the walls for the entire length of the tunnel. But even with that it seemed dimly lit. I still had to have the lights on in my car the whole way."

Marti walked past and placed down a glass of cool iced tea. She laughed and slightly shook her head, surprised that I didn't know about the tunnel. "After all," she said. "You had the cottage your whole life."

They told me how the tunnel was used often after the war. The government opened it up to the public and lake locals loved to take the shorter route. Unfortunately, by the early 1960s it deteriorated so much that it was no longer safe and they had to close it down.

"You can see the opening if you knew where to look. It is overgrown with grape vines and the bricks have weathered away," he said.

It was now after 10 p.m. and the sun had gone down hours earlier. It was too dark to paddle my kayak back home, so Marti drove me home in her car. I felt ready to

## TUNNEL UNDER THE LAKE

burst at the seams, anxious to scoop my family with this unbelievable yet true story, but I would have to wait until morning to tell them.

∽∾

The sun was bright at 9 a.m. the heat already starting to creep into the coolness of the morning. I was ready to go as I hopped on my bike and strapped on my camera to document to this historical event. Off I went down the road with my blue bicycle, blue helmet and dark sunglasses, determined to find the tunnel. The lake is about 17 miles around and I would often ride my bike on short trips, so going about five miles to find the tunnel wasn't out of the ordinary. I searched for a while, but I couldn't remember how far away the road was so I pulled over and called Bob.

"You must have just passed it," he said with a confident tone. "See if you can find it on the other side of the lake. That entrance is much larger."

"Okay," I said with a little disappointment. I peddled on and enjoyed the sun and the lake breeze. About six miles later I pulled over and dialed my father's number. I was too excited to wait any longer.

"Do you know anything about a tunnel that was dug under the lake?" I went on in great detail, bragging all about my find. "Really?" I said "You have not heard?"

Farther down the road I had another rest stop. I relaxed and sipped from my cool water bottle while I sat

## SOLD AS IS

under a large cottonwood tree. With determination I made four more phone calls, I even left messages to spread the word of my recent discovery. Each call was similar. My voice bragged," I know something you don't know. Did you know about a tunnel that was built under the lake?"

I was distracted by the lake activity and didn't notice that I must have ridden past where the tunnel should have been. I didn't really want to go back and look. It didn't matter. I was a believer. I completed my ride around the lake and wheeled back into Bob's driveway. I screeched my brakes, dripping in sweat from the humid ride. It takes a lot of energy being an adventure seeker and reporter all in one morning. I proceeded to update Bob on my inability to find the tunnel. I told him about my cell phone calls and how I chastised my friends and family because they didn't know about this piece of lake history.

Then it happened: From across the table, Marti smiled and winked at Bob. He looked straight down at the table in a feeble attempt to keep from laughing.

"What's going on?" I asked, but I didn't need an answer. I had been sucked into Bob's vortex of story tales.

Now I was guilty of being gullible. I had fallen for Bob's loon calls. There was never a tunnel under the lake. I was just knee deep in folklore and urban legend. I joined with them and laughed at myself.

I should have smelled something fishy about his tall tale. I was so intertwined in the story I never even asked Bob why the government needed to get on the other side

## TUNNEL UNDER THE LAKE

of the lake in such a hurry. Or why they had to move supplies when there is no army post anywhere near the lake. In this story, I did not disappoint him. I was reeled in hook, line and sinker.

# Contractor Blues

---ornament---

*"I will not let anyone walk through my mind with their dirty feet."*
Mohandas Gandhi

Because the cottage was far from what I dreamed it would be one day, I had a long process of renovating ahead of me. Unfortunately, I couldn't do much of this on my own and my family could only help so much, so I had to rely on contractors to assess the cottage and let me know what would need to be done. I learned quickly that they had a difficult time seeing its full potential the way I did.

It was February 2008 and we were in the midst of a cold snap. A stiff wind blew off the frozen lake and as I waited for a contractor inside the cottage the thermometer registered single digits. The chill was amplified as I trembled, unable to stay warm very long without a heat

## SOLD AS IS

source. When the soles of my feet went numb I retreated to the car to thaw out.

The structural engineer I scheduled was Paul, who was about 50 years old. His new blue jeans and baseball cap seemed out of place as he stepped through the front door. He rubbed his gloves together and stomped his feet to knock off the clinging snow, then chuckled as he noticed the small snowdrift that had formed on the wooden floor in the living room.

Paul was hired to inspect the foundation and evaluate the cottage's structural integrity. He stood in the living room and looked at the walls, noting that they lacked insulation or drywall. Then he pulled out his silver flashlight and shined it around to look closer, running his wrinkled hands along the walls to find the imperfections and weak areas.

I heard a motor humming in the distance and snow cracking under tires as it pulled into my driveway. My brother Glenn jumped out of his gray salt-stained Ford and scurried through the door. He was my oldest sibling, a decade my senior and a jack of all trades. He knew I didn't have a clue about construction so he offered to meet with the structural expert and help me make decisions.

"Where to start," Paul said as he tapped his chin and scanned around the room. "Some of the exposed beams across the kitchen ceiling are cracked. The living room ceiling is sagging like it was a hammock with someone in it."

## CONTRACTOR BLUES

"The upstairs floors shake and bounce just like a trampoline," I added.

He had a difficult time as he tried to warm his fingers so he could sketch out some basic construction designs for me. Glenn and Paul took close to an hour to brainstorm the various options to remedy the multitude of problems. When Paul finished the inspection he said he would have to complete additional research back in his office, then would draw up detailed plans and call me. I waited two weeks, but heard nothing from him after I left numerous messages and sent e-mails. With no response back I knew he was not up for my cottage transformation challenge.

During March and April the cottage was like a revolving door of potential contractors and engineers. After seven hopefuls came and left with nothing to show for it, I became somewhat dismayed. Like Paul they talked about a lot of big plans but never seemed to follow through. So when a highly recommended contractor agreed to meet one day at 5 p.m. I was optimistic. He arrived about a half an hour after I did, his car creeping down the driveway like he was unsure this was the correct address. He extended his neck out the window and peered at the numbers on the door. He was not much over 40, with blonde hair that started to recede from his forehead. He had an air of being superior with his stocky six-foot build and a shirt that hung out of his pants. Because he was a highly sought after carpenter, I was not swayed by his demeanor.

"Call me Peter," he said as he walked inside.

## SOLD AS IS

I smiled and nodded. He was quite a contrast from the down-to-earth person I heard about from those who praised him. I gave him a tour of the cottage while I explained the vision of my preliminary design. He stopped and leaned back against the wall, taking a stance that was almost standoffish as he rubbed the stubble that covered his chin.

"Whoa," he said in a condescending tone. "What you want completed is pretty extensive. Have you really looked into this?"

I didn't answer, so he continued on.

"Do you really understand what this all entails?" his voice trailing higher as he chuckled.

I wanted to phrase my answer carefully but it took me a moment. I looked down at the yellow linoleum then raised my eyes slowly as I gave a weak nod.

"No," I said. "I don't have any experience with construction. But I plan to hire professionals to guide me with the process."

Then I told him I could spend $25,000. I was not going to take out a loan.

"No way would that amount of money even come close!" he said as his smile went flat. "What you want will cost you a small fortune, at least $60,000 dollars. You want a new kitchen from the ground up, a bathroom with a shower, a storage room and the entire house rewired. In addition strengthen the structure, lay new plumbing, insulate and drywall the floors and walls, replace all the

## CONTRACTOR BLUES

windows and doors along with new ductwork and a furnace. You won't be able to do all that. The only good things in this cottage are the studs and the walls. It might as well be a new build."

I sat still and tried not to react. My face felt flush. By his reaction I knew he was skeptical of my dream, but he would not dissuade me.

"I would encourage you to just tear it down and start over," he offered in a softer tone. "You could purchase an inexpensive house similar to the ones the people lived in after Hurricane Katrina. They are clean, neat and small. It would get moved here and it's already done."

His tone bothered me and I started to feel inadequate. His negativity was too much. I softly smiled from behind my sunglasses, then thanked him for his time and walked him to the door.

It was overly evident we didn't possess the same vision. A Katrina house didn't have my family memories. It wasn't built by my ancestors and passed down through the generations. It was important to me that the renovation would follow the previous footprint and preserve as much of the past as possible. He thought that was a fairy tale. I knew any negative attitudes I had about the contractor would not help in my goal toward success. He only saw insurmountable financial obstacles while I recognized an opportunity to be creative, where I would have to discover my own gifts and knacks for doing things.

I was seeking out people not just willing to support me

## SOLD AS IS

but who also shared in my dream of the fact that the cottage was something very worth saving. From then on my life would be like a filter, accepting only positive energy and discarding anything detrimental. My desire to get my dream house would have to be stronger than any contractor's opinion. That would be my ticket to success.

# Design the New Cottage

*"Imagination is more important than knowledge."*

Albert Einstein

Optimism settled in after I sold my comfortable house in the suburbs. It was May 2008 and now I owned lakefront property and a seasonal cottage in need of intensive maintenance. Others may have seen an old cottage past its prime, but I envisioned a vibrant, updated space. In order for my construction plans be effective I had to work hard to release any constricting thoughts. I couldn't be locked into the old walls that would limit the imagination that I saw as my biggest strength.

I struggled when it came time for the actual renovation design, though. It was as if I had a blank canvas before me, and the possibilities were intimidating. I wanted to be faithful to the spirit of the original footprint but

## SOLD AS IS

still incorporate my own style. I began to read books on construction and cottage design, a project that took me way outside my comfort zone. There was little room for error—I didn't have extra funds to do rework so it was critical that everything was correct the first time.

I spent a month sorting through design magazines and filling a folder of ideas. I would sit evenings and visualize the comforts of the completed project. I could feel the heat from the new fireplace and the steam from a new shower. I pictured the cottage colors each with a personal meaning—vibrant yellow to reflect the sun, dark and light blues for the water, the green shades of seaweed and tans of the sand and stones.

I felt elated, filled with an overwhelming desire to complete my childhood dream. I didn't know how it would happen but I was convinced the vibrations I gave off would attract someone with the same enthusiasm.

Luckily I had the support of many friends who gave me wonderful suggestions that could only come from an outsider's perspective, people who could step away and not see the cottage as some kind of unchangeable family heirloom. My friends Marti and Bob rose to the challenge when I asked for their help in designing the kitchen, bathroom, storage room and living room. Marti enjoyed watching home designing shows on TV and had a knack for interior decorating. Bob, her husband, had previous experience in construction. Together they were my dream team. Marti walked silently around the small living room,

## DESIGN THE NEW COTTAGE

scanning every inch as she studied the potential. She analyzed the traffic pattern and measured the rooms to calculate the square footage.

"The flow of the kitchen into the living room doesn't work," she said. "It's cumbersome. How about you move the kitchen door over five feet, then cut a hole through the living room wall to create a new walkway?"

She pointed to the door and showed me how the change would now allow us to see the lake through the back door. The new traffic pattern would go through the side of the kitchen and the living room rather than directly through them. In the old walk way opening we could build half a wall and create a lunch bar that faces the lake.

The three of us sat down on the porch and rocked in our chairs while she drew up the final touches. I brought a pitcher of iced tea and listened to Marti clank the ice cubes against the glass while I studied the designs. After a moment a stunned look flashed over my face. For all the work I had done to free myself of the constraints of the past, I couldn't bring myself to accept such a drastic change.

"No, I can't do that," I said to Marti, thinking out loud as I shook my head.

Their suggestion was way out of my comfort zone, so my initial reaction was to deny it. With a stroke of her pen Marti had created a new space, but it was a major change. I struggled to overcome my fear of changing the cottage, of the possibility of offending my family by altering the

## SOLD AS IS

place they held so dear. I took a few days to reflect upon her suggestions. I realized that we are all afraid of different things, and I was afraid of erasing the cottage's past. As my thoughts evolved I realized how faithful the changes were to the spirit of the cottage. I decided I would move the doorways to improve the flow of the room, and by doing that I also opened my mind to let new and exciting ideas flow in. Eventually I came to see the cottage the way my friends did—as teeming with potential, not a rigid place I could not change.

# Meet the Code Officer

Uncertain of the hour, I glanced over at the clock. It was 4 a.m. I had a potpourri of emotions all stirred up inside from excitement to anxiety, all contributing to my fitful sleep.

It was the first week of May 2008, and in less than six hours I was scheduled to meet with the town code officer. He would notify me of what building permits I needed to start my renovations. He could be the most feared man in town, brandishing the power to stop your dream if it doesn't meet his standards or if his inspection uncovered major structural flaws. I was fearful of the scenarios that circled around in my mind, that it would take significant amounts of money to renovate within the codes or disapproval because I bought it without a home inspection.

I spotted him and opened the door before he knocked. My concern showed in my face. I was quiet and not my

# SOLD AS IS

normal optimistic self. Mr. Bernard was tall and thin, in his early sixties. He reminded me of a grandfather, gentle but firm. With a hearty handshake he asked me to call him James. With his neatly trimmed sandy brown hair and new polo shirt, he was quite the contrast of the contractors who passed through the cottage doors.

He walked around slowly, quiet and reserved. He paid attention to the structural details, his eyes roaming from the ceiling to floor. He studied the kitchen and then cautiously walked upstairs and stood in the bedroom. The only sound I heard was the creaking of the floor boards beneath his feet.

"When did you install this French door?" he said while he took a step forward and ran his fingers along the new frame work.

"The original door was over 80 years old," I explained as I glanced at his blue eyes behind his glasses. "It was rotted and leaked water. I just replaced it a couple of weeks ago."

"This is a code violation," he said in a deep voice. "With the door opening onto the porch roof, you will have to put up a railing, but before that occurs you have to replace the rotted floor boards, install new porch posts then strengthen the floor. Until it gets completed you will have to make the door inoperable by nailing it shut."

I folded my arms across my chest and shifted my weight back and forth on my feet. I nodded with him in agreement. He was the only code officer ever to step

## MEET THE CODE OFFICER

foot in the cottage and he could probably find a litany of violations.

"So what do you think about my project?" I asked.

He thought for a moment, tilted his head and gave me a slight smile.

"It looks like this will be a fun project. Many of the cottages this size are just ripped down and replaced with larger modern homes. You do have some barriers such as space issues, but it could be fixed up nicely. I have a cottage similar to this on the west side of the lake. I also renovated my cottage to make it more modern."

"What are you doing the next two months? Can you help?" I pleaded.

We laughed together. He was glad he wasn't doing the construction, I was glad he was laughing. It was a mutual relief. That was my first big step. The code officer closed one door but opened up another for me to enter the construction world. With his unwavering optimism I felt as though a tremendous weight had been released. To find someone who shared my vision after the revolving door of contractors was a validation that I would succeed.

I started my planning.

The cottage during the winter of 2008.

In May 2008 the renovations begin with the moving of the kitchen door.

In June 2008 the original kitchen is demolished and awaiting to be discarded.

In August 2009 the cottage is painted a tropical yellow and truck loads of soil established lawns.

# Laying the Foundation of Change

After months of interviewing contractors for the major renovation projects that still remained, my search culminated the first week in May. I just clicked with David the carpenter. He was polite, friendly and optimistic—all the important things I looked for in a contractor. He was patient as he explained his construction plans, bringing it down to a level I could easily digest. The old kitchen would be dismantled along with the bathroom and we would create a utility room for a furnace, hot water heater and washer and dryer. He would expand the current bathroom, add a shower and finish off with a ceramic tile floor. David planned to start on May 15 and be completed by June 15.

After he looked over the cottage and got everything ready it was time for demolition day, David's favorite

## SOLD AS IS

aspect of the renovation. He pried and pulled out nails with his crowbar, bringing the bathroom walls crashing down. The reciprocating saw chewed through beams and he shredded boards into splinters. The countertops and sinks were tossed out into a pile and he played tug-of-war with the unforgiving copper plumbing. After eight hours, David was weary as he completed his work for the day.

After he left I stood in the kitchen in silence, years of memories flooding by. My eyes scanned the room and stopped on the large weathered wainscoting cabinets that lined the walls. There I stood, caught between the cottage's past and the future I was building for it. I became sentimental, feeling uneasy. I would be responsible for starting a new chapter, one that took the original cottage and transformed it into something new.

It was a humbling experience knowing I had changed the family cottage forever. Through weddings, honeymoons, graduation parties and deaths it remained the same: rustic and dark yet still familiar, comforting. It overflowed with hand-me-down mattresses, old silverware and broken grills. Nothing could be thrown out until it was verified it was irreparably broken and couldn't be patched back together with wire or duct tape. Even in its worn state the cottage was still strong enough to handle the wear and tear from countless kids and pets. Feeling in tune with the moment, I turned up the music and grabbed a hammer and chisel, pounding and ripping out the large shelves and cabinets. The song was "Hero" by Mariah Carey, and it

## LAYING THE FOUNDATION OF CHANGE

sounded as if the lyrics had been written exactly for my situation. She sang about looking inside your heart, finding the inner strength to conquer your fears. The words resonated as I continued to work on the cottage by myself—"Dreams are hard to follow/But don't let anyone/Tear them away."

Two days into the project, David called and said he would have to tear up the kitchen floor. He explained that even though the land beneath the cottage sloped downward toward the lake, there was still not enough room to install the plumbing. He would have to create a subfloor from plywood. This was not part of our original construction timeline and wasn't included in the budget. With my elbows on the desk, I pulled out a small calculator and figured out that the change would cost about $1,500 and set us back a week. It also meant I wouldn't be able to refinish the original hardwood floors I desired. I couldn't control the circumstances, only accept the direction I was forced to go. I was still a bit unsure whether the decision was the right one, but I was soon ready to jump back into action, which I took as a sign I was doing the right thing.

Less than a week later David arrived at 7:30 a.m., early by his standards. He hobbled in through the door and crouched over as we made our way to the wooden bar stools at the countertop. He jotted down some figures from his weekly bill, then looked up and raised his eyebrows.

"I pulled my lower back muscle," he said. "I can't work for a while until it heals."

## SOLD AS IS

I could see the painful expression on his face as he leaned forward and started to fidget. He rubbed his lower back and tried to stretch, then winced in pain. David healed at home for over a week and the end date for the project was pushed to the 3rd of July.

When the work did finally re-start I watched from the living room as the kitchen floor came up bit by bit. The sledgehammer banged, loud creaks erupting from the splintered boards. Huge piles of red pine were tossed out the front door haphazardly, waiting to be discarded. A feeling of sadness crept over me and I filled with nostalgia. This pile of splintered wood represented my life for the next six weeks an inner turmoil that consisted of torn out memories and torn up emotions.

To add to that, the cottage became overrun with clutter. The furniture in the living room was stacked to the ceiling with only a small winding trail to pass between rooms. It looked like a garage sale with the new sinks, microwave and cabinets intertwined with the old stove, wine cabinet, table and chairs. Just like my life, the new and the old were colliding.

As we hit certain milestones our progress had to be routinely inspected by the code officer. David wheeled into the driveway one warm June morning anxious to get past a major hurdle on the project. He had jacked up the structure, strengthened and leveled the floors to prevent any additional sagging or shifting, but now it would need to get approval from the code officer. He would inspect the foundation,

## LAYING THE FOUNDATION OF CHANGE

and because my floor joists were made from wood with no cement foundation there was a high risk of rotting or insect damage underneath. The code officer walked in looking very professional and authoritative. He knelt down on the plywood as he looked between the floor joists.

"David, have you seen any rotted wood or termite damage?" he asked.

I was hoping my parents were right when they said at the closing the cottage didn't have termites. I had heard terrible infestation stories from people who thought their graphic tales of misfortune somehow helped you feel better about your situation. They never do. This was one of the few moments in the renovation that fear gnawed at me for a few minutes. The foundation would either pass or cost additional thousands of dollars to repair.

"No, it looks clean," David answered with no hesitation in his voice." I don't see any rotted boards or insect damage. The floor was in good shape, nothing I would be concerned about."

We just passed one of the most important tests in the entire construction. That night I realized I needed to release my emotions that were changing as fast as the renovations. So the next day I walked swiftly down the lake road as I listened to Christopher Reeve's book *Nothing is Impossible*. He talked about our choices in life, that we can live with self doubt and be afraid to take risks but, that life would not be acceptable. I began to feel energized to create my own dreams.

## SOLD AS IS

I practiced yoga daily and listened to inspirational speakers to help keep me balanced. I began to look inward and found more focus. Major decisions came each day and I had to be able to stay calm while everything was in disarray around me. Not one room in the house was completed, but my dreams for the cottage and my passion to make them come true were fully formed.

The original kitchen was surrounded by dark worn wainscoting.

Ellen is pulling up the linoleum floor while she is reflecting upon the past.

Empty kitchen

The kitchen floors were torn out leaving only floor joists.

Ductwork was installed,
electrical panel box upgraded,
then the ceiling was strengthened.

The lunch bar was created
from the original walkway opening.

The renovated kitchen took shape with a new floor, drywall, windows, lighting and cabinets.

The finished kitchen has nautical blue walls, a chair railing and white cabinets.

The lunch bar was designed to overlook living room along with a beautiful lake view.

# Lake Lore: Brown Station Wagon

If I was going to include a photograph that conveyed my history at the lake, it might begin with my siblings and I piling into the car and calling out to reserve our favorite seats. My four brothers, sister and I were ecstatic. Our eyes would light up and twinkle with just four simple words, "Going to the lake." As a young child I wiggled back and forth in the car seat feeling the anticipation of Fridays in the summer. We lived on the dairy farm that my ancestors had owned and twice a day Dad milked an average of fifty black and white Holstein cows. Just like it was for them, the cottage was our place of rest.

Our journey was much faster and easier than my ancestors who traveled via a brown horse and buggy. We had a 1968 Chestnut Brown Chevy station wagon. The hour long car ride would pass quickly as we played car games

## SOLD AS IS

like holding our breath when we went past a graveyard or punching arms whenever we saw a Volkswagen. Frequently we stretched our heads out the window to feel the warm breeze that blew against our faces. As we approached the lake we would have a contest to see who could see the water first. Cries sounded out of, "I see the water first." "I see the sheriff's boat." When the weather was not favorable, "I see white caps, I bet it will rain." Since all of us were first to spot something, we would all claim victory at the same time while we laughed with big toothy smiles.

Through a maze of untrimmed maple trees, the family station wagon eased down the undefined dirt driveway. Just seconds after the car engine turned off slam, slam, the car doors would ring out. Excitement was building. As our sneakers pounded the destination was the path leading to the water. We raced each other to the shore and on the narrow weathered dock. We stopped and scanned around the water with wide open eyes, trying to notice something new. The updates would be announced to no one special.

"The seaweed has gotten longer,"

"The dock looks like it is going to fall in. Don't stand there."

"I am driving the boat first."

My mother yelled down to the shore from the car, to anyone that would listen, "Carry your stuff in from the car." My Dad or brothers would build a fire in the fireplace and we would then play board or card games. The one thing we didn't miss was having a television. We would

## BROWN STATION WAGON

create our own adventures and stories to tell.

One of my first memories of the lake was when I was around five, with long blonde hair, blue eyes and full of spunk. In the early afternoons my mother cradled me in her arms and stepped carefully up each step to the top of the stairs to put me down for a nap. I was disappointed. I was the youngest and the only one forced to miss out on the fun. I listened to my mother softly walk away. As she pulled the door half closed, I crawled out of my white crib. I would stretch to stand high with my tip toes with palms pressed against the glass panes in the French doors, my oval eyes wide staring out to the water. Sleep was far away. I was longing to be watching the flurry of activity of my brothers and sister while they swam and splashed around the dock. But within minutes, unable to fight my heavy eyelids, a contented sleep would overcome me.

My most vivid memories of those summer trips were of playing in the sand and rock pile by the water, pretending I lived there and that summer would last forever. I tenderly lifted up round rocks while I hunted for tin colored crayfish. I would pick them up and study their long black bug eyes. Suddenly they would tuck their tails under dart backward and swim away. I would be the first one in the water and last one out, my hands white and shriveled from the hours soaking in the soft lake water.

With my bright red Styrofoam bubble strapped to my back like a turtle shell, I was content just floating around trying to swim. I had great memories of swimming. I

## SOLD AS IS

pulled on the mask and fins and I was just like one of the fish. Watching the fish swim by and stare at me, I thought they probably wondered about my world.

I laid on the dock on my stomach gazing down into the water, mesmerized by the flurry of activity: the brown oval clams, small crayfish, the green sunfish and striped perch. The seaweed with many varieties of shades of green flowed back and forth with the critters. They all lived together in harmony just like an orchestra moving in unison while they swayed to the music of the water. I wondered what the fish talked about and how fortunate it was that they had a whole lake in which to swim. I even felt disappointed that I couldn't breathe underwater and be part of their world.

# Lake Lore: Waterskiing

Waterskiing was a big part of my development, a sport that I loved ever since I took my first ride as a five-year old. It may be unnatural for us humans glide on top of the water, but I am all right with not being natural.

I can still vividly remember that first ride on top of my father's wide wooden skis and my arms tightly wrapped around his strong legs. He struggled to keep the skis upright as he balanced my extra weight. We would ski back close to the dock then let go of the rope as we gently slowed down and sank into the water. It was a wonderful a memory.

The first time I attempted to water-ski alone I was around seven years old. I wore small blue wooden skis that were tied together at the tips with bailing twine, to

## SOLD AS IS

hold the skis together as I was pulled on top of the water. My brother Glenn stood behind me in the water and lifted my life jacket to help me stabilize as the waves lapped at me. I wrapped my fingers around the handle and leaned back. As the boat started to tug it pulled me forward and I landed on my belly. No one explained to me when I should let go of the rope so I held on even tighter as the boat pulled me straight under the water. I thought that any second I would pop to the surface and miraculously ski. My head bobbed up and down as I traveled underwater like a fish. Just before I drowned, I finally surrendered and let go in defeat.

The next summer my balance was more finely tuned as I popped to the surface and glided along on top of the water. I was wobbly but elated as I discovered a whole new world. As I skimmed across the silver liquid I could see the water colors change from the waves that created ripples and bubbles splashing out in my wake. With the smell of the clean air, hearing the screech of the seagulls and the hum of the motor, I was hooked. As I grew older I would prefer to use a slalom ski and perform tricks, but I craved skiing on just about anything from a round disk to a knee board.

This love of skiing continues for me. A perfect example is one summer day when I skipped along as I grabbed my slalom ski and 75 feet of twisted blue and white nylon rope. My legs danged from the dock while I squeezed my feet into the ski boots and with a firm click snapped my

## WATERSKIING

life vest shut. I was ready. I stood in about four feet of water and gently leaned back, attempting a start in a standstill position.

My friend Michael sat in the back of the boat. His job was to give the driver a play-by-play accounting of my skiing and communicate by a series of hand signals. A thumbs up and the boat would go faster, thumbs down slower. A hand that went across the neck was the signal to turn the motor off. An index finger that made a circular motion in the air then pointed back to shore was the signal for "one more loop then back to the dock." He had to pay attention and inform the captain if I wiped out.

As the boat slowly inched forward, Michael threw the ski rope. I held the ski handle like a baseball bat but parallel to the ground. I leaned back and tried not to sink down, my heart racing as I anticipated the pull of the rope.

"Okay, hit it!" I yelled. The motor revved to a fast squeal, smoke puffing from the engine. The boat created enough force to pop me right out of the water. I shot thumbs up as the boat reached cruising speed of about 25 miles per hour.

With my arms straight and strong, I bent my knees to absorb the shock and felt balanced and stable while my back foot steered my ski. I leaned back and was able to crisis-cross and zig-zag over the deep wave the boat created. I pulled on the worn yellow handle and the boat pulled back, like a tug of war I would never win. The wind whipped through my blonde hair that now felt like straw.

## SOLD AS IS

I decided to do some tricks. I placed the handle of the rope in back of my knees and balanced it with both legs, and then I stood tall as I felt the pull from my knees. My hands now free in the air, I bent down and skimmed my fingers along the top of the water. I leaned side to side as I glided along. It was a challenge and yet I felt energized as I passed in front of the cottage. I let go of the rope and sank down into the water. My breath was labored and my body tired, but I couldn't wait to go again.

# Lake Lore:
# Crash Goes Grandma

"Watch out, Grandma!" my brother Brian screamed at the top of his lungs.

Our Grandma was in her late 70s, a proper British woman who commonly wore high end designer suits. She was strong-willed, beloved....and about two seconds from plunging into the lake.

It was a warm sunny day in August 1985, and there was a flurry of activity at the lake. We were thrilled feeding the ducks and catching crayfish to race. Grandma carefully walked onto the weathered dock to see all the action. The dock was slightly wobbly and unstable because it rested on top of wooden saw horses, so Grandma stood cautiously while she engaged in conversation with the multitude of swimming grandchildren. She was very supportive and enjoyed watching the waterskiers

## SOLD AS IS

maneuver and show off their new tricks.

At this time, my brother Glenn was 29 years old, he was at the prime of his pseudo professional waterskiing career. I was an envious spectator at 20 years old, watching him show off and perfect his techniques. Out in the lake he would perform spins, jumps and hold the ski rope in back of his legs. For his biggest trick, he started on a slalom ski from knee deep water then skied back to shallow water, jumped out of his solitary ski and dashed up onto the shore. If he could stay dry from the knees up he deemed it a success.

That was the plan, but sometimes plans don't go exactly as expected. After Glenn pulled on the ski dad accelerated the motorboat. Once the rope was tight he effortlessly burst above the waves and skimmed on top of the water. With precision balance he shifted his weight and jumped over the wide wave that trailed the boat. He held the rope with a strong grip but kept his body loose to absorb the bumps from the waves. I stared in awe and studied his special grip around the handle and his complex technique of jumping the waves. I idolized Glenn and his waterskiing talent.

Correct timing was critical for him to perform his audacious stunt. As Glenn curved around in back of the boat he realized he did not have enough speed and the only way to go fast enough would be to create a pendulum effect. He leaned back into his ski and zoomed to the other side of the boat, then turned and

# CRASH GOES GRANDMA

leaned in the opposite direction.

As he dropped the rope handle he realized he had over calculated his momentum and was catapulted out of control toward the dock. Grandma stood right in the middle of Glenn's path of destruction. I stared in disbelief and tried to yell, but the loud motor drowned out my squeal.

"He is out of control," my siblings yelled, stricken with horror.

Grandma nodded quickly as her eyes grew wider. She paused her conversation amidst the chorus of loud cries and looked up to fix her eyes on Glenn, but didn't have enough time to react. A split second later it was over.

Crash, splash and water flew in all directions. Glenn hit the dock. Grandma was knocked off balance and the dock swayed and dipped into the water. Her mouth flew open and with a proper scream, she reached for the empty sky to steady herself. With nothing to grab hold of she plunged into the lake ungracefully creating a giant splash. We ran and swam to her side. Her tan glasses sank to the bottom of the lake and my brother Brian dove down to retrieve them. Grandma was shaken, stirred and wet, but not hurt. With my mother's help she scurried gently back to shore. Her beauty parlor hair was matted and water dripped from her designer dress. She vowed to get back at Glenn but once safely on the porch with her towel Grandma showed a slight smile and we knew she was only joking.

Glenn was mortified at what happened and tried to maintain his composure as he stifled a laugh. Once he

## SOLD AS IS

found out she was okay he couldn't help but show a mischievous smile.

I decided that day my inexperience in waterskiing was just fine. I didn't ever want to be "as spectacular as Glenn."

Just another day at the lake.

# Lake Lore: Snowmobiles on Thin Ice

Adventures on the lake were not exclusive to the summer months, the winter held its own dangers.

"Help! Help!" The cries grew more frantic. My fear intensified as my throat narrowed.

Earlier that day the lake was much calmer, the ice dotted with colorful little tent-like shelters just big enough to fit one fisherman to sit staring at a plate size hole. They spend the day there in anticipation of a catch of a nice dinner of bluegill or perch. The wind whistled from the south. It was a cold, clear late December day in 1978. Our family rode snowmobiles often and at 1 p.m. six of us set out eager and ready for adventure on the frozen water.

My father and brother discussed the ice thickness with a neighbor who lived on the lake year round. There had been a cold snap, the temperatures hovering in the teens all

## SOLD AS IS

week and single digits at night. They agreed that with the ice thickness of six to eight inches it must be safe.

In the lead was the Arctic Cat snowmobile. It held my brother Glenn and Amy, who were newly married and anxious to start their lives together. The middle snowmobile—a luxurious heavy machine—carried my parents. My brother Barry and I were last on the older yellow Ski Doo. I held him tight around the waist. This was my first time snowmobiling on the ice and I was a little apprehensive, but overall I felt safe.

The lake was miles of white and gray ice, dotted with patches of gentle snow drifts. With the ice being so smooth, acceleration was effortless as we glided along. Sets of wide eyes scanned the horizon from behind the goggles and we peered into vacant summer houses. Glenn and Amy sped far ahead, sliding around like a ride at the amusement park while they did acrobatics on the ice.

As we approached the middle and deepest part of the lake, our group was spread out about 50 yards apart while we followed each others' tracks in the snow. What we couldn't see was the stream that drained into the lake leaving a trail of warmer water that made the ice above it much thinner. The snow that covered the ice acted as a blanket of insulation, making the ice a lot less solid than the areas around it.

Then it happened. The ice cracked and quickly gave away. I looked up to see only two snowmobiles and a set of tracks leading to a ragged hole 10 foot in diameter

## SNOWMOBILES ON THIN ICE

filled with black water. Glenn and Amy had been swallowed up in the hole after they plunged through the ice into the fridgid water. The snowmobile Glenn and Amy rode on quickly sank straight down 65 feet to the bottom of the lake. Seconds later the two helmets bobbed as they swayed back and forth, struggling to stay buoyant above the water. I knew instantly their lives were in danger.

My Dad and Barry drove up then turned off the engines about 50 feet from the hole. The scene was eerily quiet except for the desperate cries for help in the open water. Dad sprang off his machine and yelled to the rest of us, "Do not move. Stay put." Frantically he ripped off his helmet and it rolled away on the slippery ice. He then lifted up the hood of his snowmobile, grasping short pieces of rope he stored there for an emergency and tied them together to increase the length. His breath was labored. As he slid his feet along the ice his legs were mimicking the motion of a cross country skier. He was extremely cautious to displace his body weight, not knowing how close he could get to the open water before he would indeed fall in himself.

While in his heightened state he listened intently for any signs of cracking or weak ice. It was difficult for him to focus on the ice sounds when the cries from the water were more intense. He spoke in a tone I had never heard before, calm but struggling to mask his intense fear. Dad was going to do all that he could to save them both before they sank under the ice.

## SOLD AS IS

He skated closer to the edge of the ice and carefully laid down on his stomach. Now being so close to the hole he had to spread his weight over the ice. He moved like a seal, pushing his arms along his sides toward the open area. I stood with my mother and Barry about 20 feet away from the scene. We were silent as we stared at the open water feeling helpless.

Amy's survival instinct took over as she thrashed to stay afloat. She unknowingly began to climb on top of Glenn, pawing at him to prevent herself from going under the ice. Her screams became shrieks accentuated with loud gasps while she flapped her arms and kicked her legs. She struggled to tread water but it was almost like she was in quicksand. The more she kicked the deeper she sank.

Glenn unfastened his helmet and tossed it onto the ice a few yards away. He turned and tried to grab Amy by her shoulders, yelling, "You have to calm down."

Dad had now crawled to the edge and was eye to eye with Amy. With both hands he reached for her but he was still not close enough. On his stomach he crawled nearer and threw the rope but it missed Amy. She couldn't take off her helmet as she thrashed around and the steamed up visor made it more difficult to see. Dad again tossed the thin twine towards the middle of the hole and spoke in a calmer voice.

"Grab the rope Amy," he said.

Dad was apprehensive that if he grabbed Amy in her frightened state she still might unintentionally pull him

## SNOWMOBILES ON THIN ICE

into the hole. Amy saw her lifeline but it was difficult to grasp the rope with her thick gloves heavy with water. Dad pulled her toward the edge of the ice but it continued to break under her body weight, making it difficult to crest the top of the ice. She was now partially out of the water, scooching up on her stomach, but needed more leverage to get on top the ice. With a determined and powerful kick she flopped onto the ice kicking off her boot as it sank quickly to the bottom of the lake. She sat on top of the frozen water for a few minutes and sobbed.

Still in the water Glenn tenderly pulled off his waterlogged gloves to give his numb red fingers more dexterity as he pulled himself on to the ice. The bitter cold was actually a benefit, helping the bulky gloves quickly freeze to the ice at the edge of the hole. Glenn was clever, reaching out of the water to use his frozen gloves as handles then gave a swift kick to help roll on to the rim of the ice. Glenn hobbled over to Amy and knelt down to her as they embraced and she sobbed on his shoulder. Their breathing was still irregular as they spoke of thankfulness and relief.

We had a brief sense of security as we sat on the ice, but the euphoria was short lived. We all realized it was critical to get back to the cottage in a hurry. They were both waterlogged, their body temperatures had fallen and hypothermia could take hold within minutes. The temperature hovered at 15 degrees so the snowmobile suits quickly froze and became crisp and solid. The frozen suits

## SOLD AS IS

did help them to retain some of their body heat but Amy's foot was completely exposed.

We had to get back to the cottage quickly but only had two snowmobiles now. The accident occurred in the middle of the lake so we had to travel the distance of about four miles. I rode with Barry and my mother. Our snowmobile was intended for one or two people and I was cramped on the back of the machine, grasping tightly onto the seat handle.

My heart raced. I knew they had just fallen through the ice with two people on their snowmobile and now we had more weight. With white knuckles I hung off the back trying desperately not to fall as I wrapped my other arm around my mother's waist. Barry revved the motor and throttled it as fast as we could tolerate. We skimmed across the ice like a stone that was skipped across the water. I scanned the ice and attempted to look ahead, searching for signs of open water or cracks in the ice. I was scared. Barry went directly to shore, and then stayed close to the bank as possible. We pulled up in front of the cottage and without hesitation, hopped off the machines and ran full speed inside where Glenn, Amy and my father were already waiting.

Once inside the cottage, Glenn and Amy still dripped cold lake water. We helped them undress and towel dry as much as possible while Barry made a fire to help warm our bodies. The heat from the fire place was not adequate, so we started the car heater to provide more immediate heat.

## SNOWMOBILES ON THIN ICE

As we sat in stunned silence for a few minutes the day's events repeated over and over in our thoughts. Once we felt warm and safe the conversation in the car poured out of our mouths, overflowing. Each of our emotions ran freely with statements of thankfulness, sprinkled with regret. During the 45 minute car ride home Glenn even expressed his grief over the loss of his snowmobile, wondering how he would ever retrieve it.

Dad said he was worried someone might see the snowmobile tracks that lead to an open hole in the ice and think someone had fallen under the ice and drowned. Dad was a man of few words and didn't like to talk on the phone, but that night he recanted and called the sheriffs office.

"I want to report an accident," he said. "We broke through the ice on snowmobiles. No one was hurt."

He could still feel the lump in his throat as he retraced each moment. In his mind he could hear and see the cries and tried to block the frightening vision.

The sheriff broke his silence with a sigh of relief. "Whew, I am so relieved that no one was injured."

In an official tone he said, "Mark the spot as best as you can. My guys will scuba dive for it in spring and use it as a training exercise."

"Okay, that sounds like a good plan," Dad agreed.

That afternoon the sheriff notified the local newspaper of the event and the next day an article was published in the Livonia town paper called "Snowmobile sinks in Conesus Lake." It described in detail the location of the

## SOLD AS IS

sunken snowmobile in the deepest section of the lake, just 600 feet from shore. That day our family was inundated with calls from friends and family curious about the details of the accident.

One call came from a local scuba diver who said the snowmobile would not be there if we waited until spring to pull it out. He felt the newspaper article was too specific, revealing almost the exact location, and would be easy for a thief to locate.

"I would bet the farm someone would definitely steal the machine," he said.

The diver said he could help pull it out for $50, but Dad offered double the amount if he could come on New Year's eve day. The diver hesitated then agreed. He listed out to Glenn and my Dad the details of the plan. He would need Glenn to re-cut the hole in the ice and recruit a crew of people up top of the ice to pull up the machine.

Three days later, the driveway filled early with about a dozen people who volunteered to help to retrieve the sunken machine, along with a half dozen onlookers. The two ice divers arrived at 8 a.m., their light tan van crunching through the fresh snow. They packed up their supplies onto a sled and pulled it out on the ice.

Glenn and my father glided along the ice, armed with three six-foot pine planks. As they neared the weak ice they gingerly laid the boards down and walked on them to redistribute the weight. They looked to shore and lined up the landmarks, then agreed they were close to the location.

## SNOWMOBILES ON THIN ICE

Glenn, still skittish from his experience three days before, heard cracking footsteps behind him and implored, "Get back!"

The other men looked around to see a rather robust friend had nonchalantly wandered too close to Glenn.

The ice in the hole had already refrozen to a thickness of at least five inches, and they would need to cut a new hole about six-feet by eight-feet then line the edges with the boards. Glenn was armed with his orange chainsaw and the sound echoed across the desolate lake as he revved it to start. It was all warmed up and ready to cut. To carve the ice, he knelt down while staying very careful not to get too close to the edge. It was slow and tricky. Chunks of ice that broke free floated like small icebergs, and with a metal garden rake he leaned forward and pulled them out then slid them onto the solid ice.

The crew of 11 men stood about 50 feet from the hole, holding the rope that would be attached to the snowmobile. When they felt spooked hearing the natural cracks and creaks from the ice they would take off like a family of mice that heard footsteps. They would drop the rope, scatter in all directions and dash closer to shore. Then minutes later once their courage was restored they would slowly walk back and pick up the rope. They laughed and mocked each other for running away from the noisy ice, but at the same time planned for what to do if one of them crashed through.

The diving team was now all ready to go. The guy on

## SOLD AS IS

top helped suit up the ice diver, then slipped on the air tank and checked his equipment. His gear was specific to cold water, but he still had to be very cautious so the air supply didn't freeze.

The scuba diver sat on the edge and grasped the life line, then pulled his mask over his face and inserted the regulator into his mouth. He plunged into the cold water feet first and when he bobbed back to the surface he signaled with his index finger and thumb together, the okay sign. He leaned forward in the dark water and with a slight splash he sank out of sight, slowly descending to the deep. They worked in tandem, the diver who went under the ice tethered to the rope while the other diver stayed above on the ice, making sure the safety line didn't get tangled.

His breath was rhythmic and each exhale created silver bubbles that looked like plates of mercury, spinning around on the way up toward the surface until they were trapped under the layer of ice. Once at the desolate bottom the diver tried to tie a rope to the front skis but the 100-foot long braided rope couldn't reach. The divers had a unique language, communicating by a series of tugs on the rope. He pulled and notified the diver on the ice that he needed more slack.

The men holding the rope walked closer to the hole to increase the length under the ice. Less than 20 minutes after he sank to the bottom, the diver broke through the surface and handed Glenn the thick rope.

While the diver was still in the open water he said,

## SNOWMOBILES ON THIN ICE

"The rope is tied on. It looks like someone just rode it right to the bottom. It is sitting straight upright."

"Pull harder on the rope," Dad spoke loudly and the men strained and leaned back, using their body weight as leverage.

The waterlogged machine put up a fight while hand and over hand they grabbed and pulled on the long rope. It came to the surface but it would not break free—the tip of the ski was stuck under the edge of the ice. With no other recourse the scuba diver jumped back in the water without his air tank to release the sled. Then both of the tips of the skis crested the surface, followed next by the entire snowmobile. Loud cheers rang out and rounds of high fives went around, Glenn gleamed as he now had his reward. The group then carefully pushed back the machine to the shore and onto a trailer.

Glenn was prepared to save the machine, already having spoken to a mechanic to get specific instructions on how to dry it out. On shore he pulled out the spark plugs, removed water from engine, and added oil. Once back home the snowmobile was put into his basement to dry out. Glenn meticulously took it apart, removed any water and replaced parts. It had sustained a broken windshield, twisted ski and the foam seat took weeks to finally dry out. He was proud to announce to all of our surprise and amazement that he had started the "Conesus Lake snowmobile" later the next day.

The family has many snowmobiles that come out at

## SOLD AS IS

every big snowfall, and over 30 years after it plunged to the lake bottom, Glenn and Amy still have the "Conesus Lake snowmobile." But the snowmobile will never again experience the feel of ice under its tracks, never to tempt fate again.

# Lake Lore: Scuba Diving— Unexpected Complications

*"Sometimes we are lucky enough to know that our lives have been changed, to discard the old, embrace the new and run head long down the immutable course. When diving we explore ourselves as much as the sea."*

Jacques Cousteau

Ever since I was a child I dreamed of being able to breathe under the water and be part of the aquatic underworld. In my early 30s I became a certified scuba diver and underwater discovery swept me from the shallow waters to deep into the bottom of lakes and oceans.

At Conesus Lake I would dive down and hunt for items that careless boaters had lost in the water. I called

## SOLD AS IS

my collection "finders keepers," a veritable treasure chest of jewelry, watches, masks, snorkels, fins and sunglasses.

I put on my full wet suit and gloves for a dive one summer day. As I hovered in the shallow water of 10 feet I marveled at the rows of seaweed that grew like crops. I passed schools of tiny fish that swam in unison, darting back and forth to safety. The sunlight reflected off the seaweed and danced from one rock to another. I floated and peered down into the nests of eggs that the mother fish protected vehemently. I felt calm in the peaceful surroundings, my form of meditation that brought enlightenment and a happiness that swept through my body.

The lake bottom dropped off after 20 feet and I was drawn farther into the depths of the alluring bottom. I was transported into another dimension, a surreal place where no cell phones could reach me and interruptions from the outside world disappeared. The bottom at 65 feet lacked sufficient ambient light, water colors were dull and gentle rolling hills of silt made formations similar to sand dunes. When I brushed against the drifts my hand sank into the depths, it looked like a sandstorm. I was part of another world that most people never have the opportunity to experience.

Out of the corner of my eye I spotted the silhouette of a large fish. I clung to the bottom, fumbling to locate my dive knife as I poised it toward the four-foot fish who without expression lumbered by, unaware of my frightful

## SCUBA DIVING — UNEXPECTED COMPLICATIONS

state. I felt silly that my irrational mind created fear of the harmless fish.

In the depths my ears became fine tuned to the muffled noises I heard outside my own rhythmic breathing. I made out a motor's propeller in the distance, hoping that the boaters noticed the red and white dive flag tethered and floating above. The metallic tea cup size bubbles floated upward each time I exhaled and disappeared on an unorganized journey to the surface.

I no longer floated effortlessly as I reached the shallows and walked toward shore. I felt the weight of gravity take hold as the outside world reappeared once again.

∽∾

Many difficult experiences ultimately transform into life lessons. This one came as I was completing a two-day advanced scuba training at Canandaigua Lake, 30 miles from Conesus Lake. In scuba diving I must have confidence in my equipment, but on this occasion mine malfunctioned. The rest of the divers with me had swam away, unaware of my predicament as I started to panic.

The training began the previous day. It focused on three aspects: a deep dive of between 40 and 100 feet, underwater navigation and a night dive. I was with a group of seven divers plus a dive master. Our first challenge was to perform navigation skills under the water. We worked together to place lines at predetermined angles and locations. As we plotted our course it was a challenge

## SOLD AS IS

to determine distance without any navigational cues or markers to orient our location, so my dive compass became critical. We had to use hand signals to communicate to each other.

We were underwater for about 35 minutes when one of the divers, Miles, acted out of character. He thrashed his arms and legs and attempted to grab another diver in his panic. He quickly popped up to the surface while he sputtered and gasped for air. We watched closely but stayed a safe distance away so he didn't pull us under. When Miles walked to shore he started to hyperventilate, and the dive master had to reassure him. The problem occurred when Miles became fatigued and accidentally gulped water, causing him to choke. We were not nervous for our safety but became aware of our own limitations. With the unexpected complications Miles was unable to complete his certification that day.

During the night dive the full moon penetrated the water through a canopy of stars, creating an eerie glow. I perched on the edge of the boat as I checked my flashlights and air level, then illuminated the glow sticks. I took a giant stride off the boat and with a splash entered the black liquid. I pointed the beam of light at my dive partner as we descend feet first. As one world closed another unfolded, beyond the tunnel of light that my flashlight created was the unknown darkness. The dark green seaweed slowly swayed back and forth as I passed it, glimmering with the flashlight rays.

## SCUBA DIVING—UNEXPECTED COMPLICATIONS

I struggled to curb my active imagination, from automatically envisioning that every shadow was attached to a dangerous sea creature. I was spellbound as I spotted a large pike looking at me eye-to-eye. The fish seemed to be suspended motionless until the beam of light flashed in his sleepy eyes and he swam away. Below me I spotted the other divers' lights as they criss-crossed and illuminated the lake creatures. The dive ended and we drove our cars away, where again the visibility only existed where the headlights shined. But I don't have any fear of what is ahead on the road, so venturing into the unknown on my night scuba dive didn't scare me either.

The final section of the course was the deep dive. The dive master described the plan—we would dive down along a pipeline, view a sunken sailboat at 90 feet then exit from a different location in a triangular pattern. The instructor warned us about not getting too close to the silt at the bottom with our flippers as this would reduce visibility.

My partner was Jeremy, an adventure seeker and good friend. We checked each other's equipment and with one turn on the knob the air flowed into my regulator. I entered the water and hovered about 10 feet from the lake's bottom. The dive master was in the lead, and since I was one of the more experienced divers in the group I was last as we descended.

My depth gauge registered 78 feet when with a strong kick Jeremy flicked his fin upward and created

## SOLD AS IS

an enormous cloud of silt. My visibility until then had been about 20 feet but as the cloud surrounded me it diminished to zero. I flashed my light back and forth in an attempt to catch Jeremy's attention, but he didn't see it. I knew the dive master planned on a triangular dive pattern, which meant they would not come back. I decided that because I wouldn't be able to locate them I would just slowly ascend to the surface and meet them back on shore.

My diving gear included a vest secured to the scuba tank and strapped to my shoulders that helped control buoyancy. When I wanted to surface I would press the inflator button to release air from the tank and transfer it into the vest. As I pressed it I heard a noise and noticed a trail of white bubbles floating upward past my head, but nothing happened. I instinctively pushed the white button a second time and still there was no change. The hose to my inflator had come disconnected. My chest tightened with a rush of adrenaline. I was trapped on the bottom of the lake all alone, my breathing the only sound against the deafening silence.

The air in a scuba tank is 79 percent nitrogen and 21 percent oxygen. The longer I stayed down at that depth the more nitrogen would accumulate in my blood and it couldn't be released until I reached shallower levels, where it is reabsorbed and breathed out. I had 15 pounds of weights in my vest to help counteract the body's natural buoyancy and I couldn't just drop my weights and pop to the surface because the safe ascending rate is 30 feet per minute. Anything faster and nitrogen could be released into my bloodstream in bubbles that would expand and cause the bends. The name comes from the fact that when these bubbles are released and settle near large joints of shoulders or legs, the diver "bends over" in pain. Excess nitrogen could cause injuries from intense pain to full-blown paralysis.

I sat on the bottom of the lake in the foot-deep silt. Seven minutes passed with my situation appearing implausible. My mind raced around the seriousness of the situation as dread filled my heart. I was now breathing faster and deeper, fighting my internal struggle as I gave in and started to cry. Heading for a full-blown panic attack my survival instinct kicked in to help conquer my fear. I calmed down and recognized that the first motto in diving was "panic kills." My fear had disoriented me, causing my mind to exaggerate the potential threat. I sat and closed my eyes as I slowed my breathing, racking my brain for a favorable outcome. Weighing the pros and cons, I came up with some possible solutions.

## Plan A.

The good part was I had air to breathe, it just couldn't enter my vest to make me buoyant. I could drop my weights and hope I was not underwater long enough to build up significant nitrogen, but that was risky. As I would get

# SOLD AS IS

shallower my body momentum would increase and release nitrogen before it could be absorbed. I had multiple dives that day and needed to decompress properly.

## Plan B.

I had enough air in my tank to swim/walk along the pipeline back to safety. Even with poor visibility, it would guide me along and prevent me from ascending too quickly. This was the best way to prevent decompression sickness. The pipeline would be my lifeline.

I felt relieved and hopeful as I initiated my plan, but just as I started to stand up I saw a flash of light then thin streaks of twinkling lights through the brown haze. The flicker became brighter until I saw the dive master approaching. I was no longer alone. I signaled to the dive master and showed him my broken equipment. He had me hold the back of his tank as he slowly rose up to 20 feet, then hovered for a five-minute safety stop to release extra nitrogen.

The divers never noticed I was missing. The only reason they came back the same way was because when they approached 90 feet the transition from warm to colder waters was too dramatic and the divers were uncomfortably cold. They abandoned the plan to exit from another location and by fluke happened to come back my way.

It is nearly impossible for humans to think rationally when we are experiencing intense feelings, including fear.

## SCUBA DIVING—UNEXPECTED COMPLICATIONS

Because of the lesson I took from that day at the bottom of the lake, I learned to step away from my heightened emotional state and once I was calm to create a solution. It was a big life lesson, one I still use whether it's for a renovation problem or some other unexpected complication.

# Unleashing my Power of Creativity

Since childhood we've heard of the people that try to intimidate dreamers by telling them if they don't know how to do something they shouldn't do it, but I disagree. We must follow our desires, even if they deliver us to unknown territory.

As adults we often tend to be fearful of being judged or scrutinized, but we can only achieve a metamorphosis when we are outside our comfort zone. If you tell yourself you can't do something, you can choose to pay attention to your inner voice or ignore it. When you are authentic with your thoughts and feelings, your imagination will expand and propel you to acquire your dream.

The small living room in the cottage had a fireplace

## SOLD AS IS

much too large for the small space, with soot-stained, yellow bricks and a warped pine mantel. This had been the centerpiece of the living room, providing lots of cozy fires and taking the dampness off rainy nights. It was my also my only heating source, and I really wanted to have a nice fire to take the chill out of the air but its condition was in question. I remembered learning at the real state closing my parents had never cleaned the chimney and I knew this needed to be done before I could use it.

Days later a white van with a picture of a chimney sweep on the side slowly crept up on the crushed stone driveway. The man inside got out, not wasting any time to introduce himself looked up.

"Wow, look at that chimney," he said cautiously.

The chimney sweep was in his 30s with wispy blonde hair and a shirt wrinkled from work. With a critical eye, he walked carefully around outside. Once inside the living room he leaned over and poked his head up the chimney opening. He pulled his head back and looked concerned but tried to sound optimistic.

"The good news is that for being 80 years old the chimney is straight as an arrow. The bad news is it can't be swept. You need major chimney repair work."

He went on in great detail, describing how the mortar was falling out along with bricks it held in place. He used a tool to pry out a brick and it fell to the floor of the fireplace. I risked starting the cottage on fire if I used the

## UNLEASHING MY POWER OF CREATIVITY

fireplace, he told me. He was debating what to say next, but I could anticipate his question.

"When was the last time it was cleaned?" I hung my head low, moving it from side to side.

Standing in the living room gazing out the old windows, I saw all the firewood that had been cut and split. This made the news especially disappointing. The property was surrounded with trees that had been cut down and would provide cozy fires for years. I loved the smell and crackle of a real wood fire, but couldn't risk having the house burn down. I decided that day I needed to install a gas fireplace.

As I walked with the man to his van to say goodbye he turned back toward me.

"You might get bats if you don't put a screen at the top off the chimney," he said.

"Really? Bats? I wouldn't want that." I replied.

The fireplace needed to be redesigned and cut down to fit the dimensions of the room. A local fireplace company came to give me an estimate on the work and said they could reduce the size with a mortar saw but only the sides. They were not comfortable cutting the top mantle section. I thought that every side would have to be cut for it to look symmetrical, plus the estimate was much higher than I anticipated. They were not right for the job.

After they drove away I walked to the porch and sat down. I was at a roadblock. When faced with renovation

## SOLD AS IS

decisions I went not with experience but my instinct, so I came up with Plan B: do it myself. Feeling apprehensive but determined, I drove to the library. The mission was to learn about cutting down a fireplace. The more information I assimilated the more my confidence grew.

The next trip was to the local hardware store. But before that, a quick shower and dress for a friend's wedding. I had on a white dress, earrings and high heels when I walked confidently up to the sales counter. This was not my domain, but I fully accepted that. A tall, lanky gentleman with an olive complexion turned around to assist me.

"How hard would it be for me to cut down a brick fireplace and what saw blades would I need?" I asked.

"You might want to change your outfit first," he said smiling with a slight chuckle.

I smiled back and shook my head. I am sure he was thinking, "I hope someone is there to call 911 when she cuts her arm off."

I wondered if it was going to be really hard or just intimidating. There was a big difference in my book, and I wasn't going to allow a self-limiting belief that it couldn't be done. Psychologists estimate that we have more than 40,000 thoughts per day. I wanted to focus only on the productive thoughts and ignore the thousands of others.

Mr. Hardware man loaded me up with the essentials: a diamond-tipped round blade for the circular saw, masks,

## UNLEASHING MY POWER OF CREATIVITY

goggles and plastic sheeting. I was ready for battle, me against the fireplace. All I would need now was an open-minded person with imagination. I wasn't going to touch the saw. They scare me.

I had the perfect person. My friend Mick loved to do side jobs, especially dirty or difficult ones. He also brought his father-in-law Ken. Mick showed up in worn out army fatigue pants. Though skeptical at first, he was up to the challenge.

Mick flashed a radiant smile and a spoke with a charming British accent.

"Can we cut down the fireplace with a circular saw?" Mick asked.

"I don't know," I said. "But the brick is solid and seems structurally sound. We have nothing to lose."

The three of us put on our dust masks, looking like we were ready to handle an infectious spill, and revved up the saw. We were ready to begin, gloves and goggles all in place.

"Let's just start cutting the bricks and see what happens," I said confidently to Mick, following my inner voice.

I was nervous I didn't know what we were getting into, but I wasn't worried. Red sparks flew, dark gray smoke puffed and a cloud of dust blew out of the bricks and filled the air. The room was wrapped in plastic to keep the dirt and dust out but it still engulfed us. Heavy thick smoke enveloped every nook and cranny and we could not

## SOLD AS IS

see each other at times. Ken and I pounded and chipped away with chisel and hammer. It was a tug of war between us and the stubborn bricks.

I was proud of Mick and Ken for being willing to try something new. It took us about two hours and when we were done we looked like we were through a war—soot all over our faces, grime, brick dust and pebbles in our hair. But we won the battle, and with no major injuries. It was by far the loudest, dirtiest project in the entire renovation.

Hours later I stood and looked at the fireplace. It was smaller and ragged, with bricks falling off the sides. I mixed up a bag of cement and started to put back the bricks that had fallen off, finishing it myself. It was only 40 degrees inside and I shivered as I worked along to the invigorating music, my determination and excitement keeping my spirit warm. I finished three hours later. Another day toward my dream of a warm, insulated, finished living room.

As I sat that night looking at the changes, I realized that cutting down the fireplace was very freeing. It represented the chipping and cutting away of the old worn cottage and replacing it with loving care, preserving it for future generations. I love the size of the new fireplace—the classic white mantel adds definition and gives extra prominence to the focal point of the room.

To complete my vision I wanted to add blue and green sea glass tile, which held special memories from a previous vacation.

## UNLEASHING MY POWER OF CREATIVITY

One summer during a visit to Cape Cod I rediscovered the wonder of sea glass myself. It is formed by glass falling overboard boats, then becoming worn down through wave action and ultimately washed up onshore.

One summer day in 2008, before the children arrived at the cottage I sprinkled additional sea glass along the shore. It had odd shapes and brilliant blues, purples, greens and browns. As soon as the kids got out of the car, they started to scour the beach and check out the water. When they discovered the glass they asked for plastic bags and containers to capture their treasures.

"Can you believe this? It is awesome," I heard one of them say.

They stacked their piles carefully, separating the colors and trading with each other for certain colors, shapes and sizes. This sea glass adventure gave them hours and hours of enjoyment. Such a small thing, but for them it had a lot of meaning and created wonderful memories.

The sea glass tiles around the fireplace was the natural substance to use. Once again my thoughts drifted and I wanted to try to do install it myself. After I hung the sea glass and spackled it, everything came together. I was elated with my new fireplace. I stood back with awe and satisfaction. It is beautiful, nautical and just what I had imagined.

A soot stained, overly large fireplace was a centerpoint in the living room.

Mick cut down the bricks to re-size the fireplace, despite the black smoke and sparks.

New windows along with a sliding glass door was installed, the weak ceiling was strengthened.

The dark red hardwood floors were refinished then insulation and drywall was hung.

A completed living room with light green walls surrounds a white mantel and sea glass fireplace.

# Shattered Dreams

*"Acknowledge that you failed, draw your lessons from it, and use it to your advantage to make sure it never happens again."*

Michael Johnson—Olympic Gold Medalist

It was a hot, muggy Saturday three weeks into the cottage renovation and the driveway was filled with vans and trucks, not a party but a gathering of contractors. The kitchen now had a plywood floor and open walls that showed the studs. The electrician was hired to install all new electrical wiring, panel box, electrical fixtures and outlets. The plumber would run drainage lines to the toilet then connect all new plumbing to the sinks, dishwasher, bathroom and washer.

I also needed someone to create new ductwork for the furnace, so I interviewed multiple heating and cooling guys. This was a difficult process, being a woman and

## SOLD AS IS

walking the fine line between telling them I know nothing and pretending to have basic knowledge. In the end I took the cheapest estimate, a man named Allen who showed up with a shirt winkled and stained with sweat. It was not my best decision.

Since I couldn't use the fireplace anymore, the furnace ductwork would help provide heat to the bedrooms and the lower house. Allen brought his 10-year-old son Jason, a cute wide-eyed kid excited to help out his Dad. I didn't like that idea that his child came with him, but I didn't say anything. I should have gone with my gut and asked Allen not to have his son help, but I didn't speak up. They would have to work in the living room already crowded with appliances and kitchen cabinets that were waiting to be installed.

I always liked the look and character of a round shower and after spending weeks looking for specials I found one at a close-out sale. It was the last one, a discontinued round shower. The shower wasn't quite ready to be installed, so it sat intermixed with all the other waiting-to-be-installed items in cardboard boxes on the floor right where Allen and his son were working.

Allen had just emptied his truck and was starting to cut holes in the ceiling and drill in the screws to hold up the ductwork. I looked out to the water when I heard someone yelling, but I couldn't tell what they were saying. I ran out to see my friends pulling their blue and white motorboat up to my dock.

## SHATTERED DREAMS

"Come out on the water with us, Ellen. Take a break," they shouted.

How could I resist? I ran back inside and bounded up the stairs to grab my favorite bathing suit and towel. I was smiling ear to ear, all too happy to succumb to peer pressure. I had been desperately craving a little rest and relaxation from all the construction stress and painting day after day. There was an overwhelming amount of work to finish and while looking at the completion of my labor was satisfying I was becoming overrun with exhaustion. After working eight hours at my hospital job, and then painting in the evenings well past 10 p.m. at night in the cottage. I felt guilty taking breaks or having fun. It was creating a new level of exhaustion and I even found myself slurring my words.

On the water I was in heaven. We went to a part of the lake where you can stand in the shallow water, floating the boat over a sandy bottom. It is a great place to socialize, where people will throw Frisbees and play with their dogs and kids. I floated in the water and celebrated life. What a wonderful day.

Hours later I was feeling refreshed and eager to see the progress. While walking up the wide gray steps on the porch, a feeling came over me that something was not right. Looking through the window of the sliding glass door, staring in disbelief, a sickening feeling flooded over me. Shattered glass was all over on the floor. Once inside I saw thousands of tiny octagon pebbles strewn in every

## SOLD AS IS

area of the living room, under the couch, in the kitchen and even on windowsills.

The kid had been standing on the step ladder pounding a pipe, a nice wide swing with a mini sledgehammer and a loose grip on the handle. These two things together spelled disaster. The hammer flew through the air and slammed into the round shower.

"Oh no, not my shower," I breathed deeply and shrieked.

As I turned around and walked back out to the water to comprehend the situation my breathing became faster and my face turned red. My thoughts started racing. Sitting on the porch and looking at the lake calmed me but my breathing still had not returned to normal.

Allen walked out to me. "Did you see what happened?" he said. "I am sorry. How much did you pay? I will reimburse you for it."

A moment later I blurted out the price, then realized the problem. It was a discontinued item and there were no more available. He was taken back by what I said and interrupted me mid-sentence.

"I don't think so," he said in a condescending tone. "Honey, I won't pay more than you did for the shower."

I felt flush, my disappointment rising. I thought he must be confused—my name was not "Honey." All I wanted was for him to buy me another shower. I asked him to leave, frustrated that I let my feelings get the best of me. I was not proud of this moment. As he left the

## SHATTERED DREAMS

house he shrugged his shoulders and said he would look into buying another shower and get back to me. I was not impressed.

He didn't have a vacuum cleaner with him so I cleaned up his mess. I was angry, disappointed and had a hard time believing it really happened. Just because I am a woman, I shouldn't be treated like I don't know what is ethical and right. I am not Honey. I felt used cleaning up the mess he created.

While I was soaking up some sun in the yellow Adirondack chair later on in the day, feeling tired and sore, the cell phone rang. It was Allen. I wasn't looking forward to talking to him but I had to resolve the problem.

"Good news," he said in a completely convincing tone. "I found a great square shower. It will be paid for. Just pick it up in the city and tell the front desk your name and our situation will be settled."

My phone almost dropped out of my hand and I nearly fell out of the chair. I was now sitting sideways trying to balance with my toes touching on the ground.

"Are you kidding?" I replied with annoyance in my voice. "I am not going to accept anything less than a round shower delivered to the same spot mine was shattered."

He said he would look into it further and get back to me. We were at a standstill. He couldn't find a round shower at a reasonable price, and I wasn't going to get a square one because of his son's negligence. Days passed. David was waiting to install the shower, and this problem

## SOLD AS IS

was holding up my whole schedule. I was so frustrated and getting more impatient by the hour. Allen ended up talking to David for advice and David said he needed to make it right, even if it cost him money.

Soon after the phone call, Allen finally did the right thing. He bought and delivered a new round shower. He came with his son and dropped it off in the living room where the other had shattered. It cost more than he was paid for the labor of the ductwork but I was finally a satisfied customer.

We both learned a big lesson that day, but in the end the right thing was done. My mistake was hiring the cheapest contractor and not checking his references. I should have listened to my gut instinct and not let the uninsured, inexperienced kid help out.

Sometimes when barriers appeared, it forced me to be more aware of opportunities to improve. When I listened to my instincts or inner voice, I realized that in order to live life to the fullest my emotional thoughts had to be in alignment with my intellectual reasoning. It was important for me to understand the difference. I discovered that inner turmoil was created when my thoughts were conflicted, however when they were in sync with my logical thoughts I became energized and decisions were clear. I reasoned it would be okay for the son to be there, but my inner feeling said it was at a great risk. My feelings were not in alignment.

Later that day while cleaning the new shower walls I

## SHATTERED DREAMS

remembered reading that Thomas Edison failed 10,000 times before he invented the incandescent light bulb. My reflections were more of a temporary defeat, not a failure. I knew I was on the right track and would not make the same mistake twice.

Weeks later I would be able to shower in my own house and not have to run off to the local health club. Such a small thing that we all take for granted was a great success to me. After my first shower, my hair still dripping wet, I walked across the porch. I just stood there, watching the boats go by and realizing just how fortunate I was.

# Rental Woes

Throughout my first summer of cottage ownership the sound of chainsaws whining was a regular occurrence. The landscape was littered with untrimmed and diseased trees and because I was on a tight budget I would do the work without hiring a professional contractor.

The mature maple, cottonwood and elm trees surrounding the property had been overgrown and filled with dead branches. One tree had a massive branch that hung far out over the water, interfering with the view of the lake. I cringed at the estimate I had received from Carl the arborist, plus he wouldn't cut it down in the summer. Instead his plan was to wait until the lake froze over in the winter and cut the limb onto the ice where he could slide it off.

So I choose to do it myself, enlisting the help of a couple of friends. Not wanting to waste a moment I grabbed

## SOLD AS IS

the paint brush and paint can. It was a hot August day and I sweltered even with the gentle breeze. I squinted into the early morning sun while I stood on the rail of the aluminum ladder. I grasped the yellow paint can in one hand and clung to the dormer roof in the other. My friend Ken pulled into the driveway to check out my progress and as I turned to greet him the paint can rolled off the roof, hitting me in the chest and sending cold yellow paint oozing down my face and chest and onto my pants. Dripping in yellow paint and laughing at my predicament, I struggled to regain my balance and not fall off the ladder. I ended up jumping into the shower clothes and all—not the best start for a day of tree removal.

To help bring down the trees I rented a 40 foot bucket lift for three days. It looked like a piece of equipment from a moon landing, with four long legs that moved individually. Mick, who had come to help with the cutting, practiced raising the bucket up and down and back and forth. For that entire first day the chainsaw blew out plumes of smoke as it buzzed and cut the trees surrounding the cottage.

On day two I noticed a brownish-red fluid dripping from one of the big arms that helped stabilize the machine. As the day wore on it became a steady drizzle so I placed a bucket under the machine to collect the dripping fluid. When I visited the man at the rental company he said he noticed the drip but thought it was insignificant. If I returned the lift to the store it would be weeks to get a

## RENTAL WOES

hydraulic specialist to replace the parts. He added that we could use it with caution, but when the fluid ran out the mechanics would seize up. To be safe he gave me a couple gallons of hydraulic fluid to keep things moving until the project was done. Throughout the day I added the lubricant as it continued to steadily drip out.

My neighbor Matt wanted to help cut tree branches. His shirt collar was open to the summer heat with just a trickle of wind to cool him off. Mick and Matt looked like professional arborists as they flexed their necks and stared up at the branch, trying to decide if the lift was tall enough to reach it. It was a risky proposition—the branch was about as wide a large person and definitely worth some respect. We invested in thoughtful planning to coax the direction it might fall. The plan was to cut small notches on the underside so it would break free and slowly fall into the water, but in the end it would fall where it wanted to.

Matt climbed into the bucket, articulated the control lever and rose slowly stopping just below the branch. We watched from below as we heard the chainsaw slicing into the wood. Saw dust trickled to the ground, followed quickly by an earth shaking crash. As it fell the branch crashed into the lift, pushing the bucket downward before it recoiled up again. Matt held on tight with the unexpected jolt then shouted a nervous "I am ok" to the spectators, but even though he was unharmed Matt was still trapped. The branch had pinned the arm that controls the lift and

## SOLD AS IS

prevented the bucket from being lowered. Matt stood helplessly 40 feet up and watched as Mick prepared his chainsaw and began removing debris so he could lower the bucket. Less than 15 minutes later the wood was cut free and the bucket lowered.

Even with the drama of the tree crashing Matt enjoyed the experience and Mick was like a kid with a new toy the way he played with the lift bucket. I would have been satisfied to never to rent a piece of equipment again. Of course that was only the beginning of my adventures in renting.

༺༻

Twenty-nine trees had been cut down, which inevitably lead to my dilemma of removing all the stumps. With the sheer multitude of them spread across the yard it would cost a small fortune to have a smooth lawn, so I decided to try something new. I rented a stump grinder. While in the rental store to pick up the grinder Thomas the owner provided instructions about the care and usage of the grinder.

It was a powerful machine with a large spinning blade and cutting teeth that could chew through just about anything. At the cottage, Mick and I adjusted our goggles and inserted our ear plugs. Mick pulled the rope to start the motor and it sprang alive. He swiveled the machine back and forth over the top of the stump as it chipped away the layers of wood. We bobbed our heads, dodging the

# RENTAL WOES

flying debris as a cloud of sawdust spread 25 feet around us. Mick turned off the motor to reposition the machine over another stump's front edge. Grasping the handle in his sweaty palms, he pulled the rope and it broke away from the machine.

"I can't believe it," he said. "It's broken."

I dialed the owner of the rental store as I started to question whether it would have been better to hire a company to grind the stumps instead of attempting it ourselves.

"It is a fairly new machine," he snapped at me. "It couldn't have just broken down on its own. What did you do to it? You are going to lose your deposit and pay to have it repaired."

"I am not going pay for the full day rental or the repair when we only worked on one stump," I exclaimed. "I only had it for half an hour!"

Mick and I loaded the heavy grinder and drove it back to the rental store. I would have preferred to delay the inevitable confrontation with the store owner but I wanted to articulate my feelings accurately. I was dumbstruck that our perspectives were at such opposite ends of the spectrum.

As I pulled into the driveway I felt tense as the owner came out to greet me, but he immediately apologized for his tone and stated that he overreacted. He said customers misuse his equipment all the time and went on to tell melodramatic stories about previous renters who

## SOLD AS IS

had demolished his equipment. There was a floor sander dropped out of a car that broke its handle in two and a backhoe that fell off a retaining wall when the operator ignored warnings. At that point our perspectives were beginning to mesh. I understood his frustration; he understood he was just reacting to those previous mishaps.

Thomas attempted to fix the stump grinder at the store and asked me to wait so Mick and I could use it again that day. It took about 45 minutes to reattach a recoil and install a new starter. His tone was genuine when he told me to keep the stump grinder as long as I needed and offered to pick it up at my house. I felt lighter as I drove away, a satisfied customer and another life lesson.

Mick and I were determined to complete our goal of eradicating every stump and after four hours he was sore and felt as though a knife was stuck in his back. He passed the grinder handle to me to take over. Despite my doubts and pains in my lower back I was determined not to quit. The twenty-ninth stump was the hardest, both emotionally and physically. We were both drained, stumbling as we swiveled the grinder around back and forth until the stump finally disappeared. Celebration flowed as I grabbed some refreshments and we lounged by the water, another typical day in the slow transformation of the landscape.

⁂

I wanted to create a new living room floor on a small budget so I decided to strip and refinish the floors myself

## RENTAL WOES

without hiring a professional. I loaded up with gallons of stripping paste to assist in breaking loose years of dark stain and lacquer that accumulated on the floors. It was a tedious process as I poured lumps of the paint stripper in a four foot area then scraped inch by inch. For days I struggled to get into the deep nooks and crevices until I discovered that the steel bristled brush worked fantastically.

After the stripping was done I was ready to rent a floor sander, but didn't know what type to choose. There were many styles and to add to my confusion the rental stores had differences of opinion. The belt sander was the most powerful but could leave ruts in the wood if it didn't stay in constant motion. The orbital and vibrating sander wouldn't get as deep in the wood, but was more forgiving for an inexperienced user.

Luckily the decision was made for me. After all my research I ended up renting the orbital sander because it was the only one available on the day of the project. I had to visit another dreaded hardware store and stood uncomfortably at the counter waiting for the sales associate to make eye contact.

"Can you show me how to use an orbital floor sander?" I asked politely. "How hard is it to use?"

Peter, a tall, stocky man in his 20s, nonchalantly demonstrated the technique.

"Simple, just put the sandpaper on the floor and lower the sander on top of the paper, then flick this switch

## SOLD AS IS

to turn it on. It is not like a vacuum, you have to keep it in constant motion. I guarantee you won't have any problems."

Once I returned to the cottage, I flung open the doors and was kissed by the cool breeze that blew through the house. I slid on my safety goggles in anticipation of creating beautiful hardwood floors, but when I flicked the switch and mimicked the previous instructions, the sandpaper spun around in a circle and flew off the machine. I must have installed it wrong, I thought. I re-adjusted the sandpaper but again had the same outcome. I put on a new piece of paper and tried it again with the same result. I couldn't believe it didn't work.

I called Peter at the rental store.

"I can't get the sandpaper to stick," I said sheepishly. "It just spins around and falls off. What do I do?"

"You must be doing something wrong. The sander worked fine yesterday when it came back from being tuned up."

He reviewed the correct operating procedure as I resisted my initial response to raise my voice. When I described what the sandpaper had done I could tell by his tone that he didn't believe me.

"I am stunned," he said. "I have never heard of any of my sanders not working. Did you drop it out of your car or something?"

A déjà' vu hit me as I thought of the stump grinder incident. I didn't answer his question, just loaded up the

## RENTAL WOES

sander and drove back to the rental store. When I arrived Peter had gone home for the day and a gentleman in his late 60s tipped his head and looked up slowly.

"I have a sander in the back of my jeep that I just rented a few hours ago and doesn't work now," I said as I pantomimed the spinning action of the sandpaper.

"You must not know how to use it," he said. "This orbital sander was just serviced last week and it worked fine. I will give you better instructions."

I felt my self control ebbing away and flinched at his condescending words. He wheeled the sander to the repair room. Vroom it started with puff of dust. He showed me the proper technique and offered suggestions on what I might have done incorrectly. I stood for five minutes receiving my lesson and waiting for him to refute me.

But then it happened—the sandpaper spun in a circle and flew off the machine, exactly as I described earlier.

"It looks like something is wrong," he said apologetically as he shifted his weight.

"Are you sure? I have been telling you that for five minutes now."

I drove to the rental store that helped me with the stump grinder, knowing I would have a better experience there. The gentleman behind the counter recognized me from when I rented the stump grinder. I told him of my experience with the broken sander from the other rental store and he reassured me his sander would work. The moment of truth came in my living room when I prepared

## SOLD AS IS

the sandpaper and it actually sanded the floor. It took me about three and a half hours to get the entire floor prepared and the day passed without any more incidents.

A week passed and as I prepared the floors they became brighter and clearer, similar to my own feelings. I realized I was uncomfortable in a hardware store and maybe they were also with me, but that didn't stop me from trying new things. In retrospect stripping and refinishing the floors was a significant decision with intensive manual labor, but I would do it again.

# Lake Lore: Flying Unwelcome Guests May 2008

The chimney sweep's warning to install screen over the chimney became reality all too soon. With tears in my eyes, I stood outside peering into my kitchen window. It was 2 a.m. and I was distraught. I remember the three words that haunted me at the real estate closing, "Sold As Is," but I didn't think that included bats. I guess the bat didn't get the notice that a new tenant had moved into her house.

I watched an ominous mother bat looking for her lost babies fly around the cottage like a race track—through my kitchen then through the living room. Whoosh, clip clip clip, she circled over and over again. It was the biggest bat I had ever seen.

My throat tightened and my chest grew heavy. I wanted

## SOLD AS IS

to cry. This black creature forced me out of my house in the middle of the night. I crawled into my jeep with the phone book and blankets in tow. I wished for sleep, but before that would happen I thumbed through the yellow pages, looked up bat removal and with a shaky voice left a message for the bat man.

He arrived before the dew was off the grass, wearing scuffed worn cowboy boots. He was a short man, reserved but friendly, and gave the impression that he routinely calms the panic of onlookers. He could have talked for hours about bats: where they live, rabies and their need for water. All I wanted to know was how to make them disappear. He walked confidently around the structure then leaned the fiberglass ladder against the chimney and sealed off the square opening at the top.

Next he sprayed foam in the nooks and crevices bats might squeeze through. It only needed to be as big as a dime for them to fit through, he told me. After searching the upstairs he was confident the mother bat had returned outside during the night. He said it was common for the baby bats to lose their way as they learn to fly and maneuver around.

The upstairs bedrooms had holes around the windows where the sunlight filtered through. Every winter we would get a small snow drift inside the living room from the open spaces. To others it must have seemed strange seeing the holes but it was just part of the cottage's special charm.

Everything was fine for a couple of weeks until one muggy late summer night. The lake waves were calm, but

## FLYING UNWELCOME GUESTS

inside the house calmness would not prevail. My sister-in-law Amy was staying at the cottage and my friend Sharon was on a visit from Phoenix for a couple of days. Out west in the desert, they have killer spiders and scorpions. Sharon thought she was safe in Upstate New York, but she was incorrect.

As I showed Sharon around her bedroom we started to reminisce and laughed but then out of the corner of my eye I saw something out of place. I focused, and then squinted. It became clearer. Hanging upside-down in the wooden rafters was a black bat the size of my fist.

I blurted out, "Bat! Bat!" We briefly looked at each other and our expression changed quickly from disbelief to utter panic.

I tried to stay rational but my heart was nearly beating out of my chest. We shrieked at the same time, then jumped back and stumbled clumsily down the stairs. I flopped onto the couch and told Amy what had happened.

"Oh no," Sharon exclaimed. "Our cell phones." We had left them upstairs.

"How do we call for help?" Sharon asked. We looked at each other, not sure what to do.

There was no way Sharon would go back upstairs, so I curbed my fear and pulled a blanket over my head. I went into combat mode, doing the army crawl slowly up the stairs. I snatched the cell phones and ran back down like a big monster was chasing me. I will admit I was scared and creeped out, walking the fine line between laughing and crying.

## SOLD AS IS

"What do we do next?" I said.

"We have to go to a motel," Sharon said after taking a moment to regain her composure.

Amy was bewildered. "No you are not. I will not stay here alone."

It would not have been fair to leave Amy there all alone—she was more afraid of the flying beast than either of us. So we decided to stay and not abandon Amy. We tried to watch TV but our thoughts drifted to the unwanted pest that flew around upstairs. The three of us stayed up as late as we could, unable to concentrate. We worried about how it might attack us the moment we fell asleep. Amy eventually slept on the blue pull-out bed by the window while Sharon and I took the other sleeper sofa.

I was on guard, with a blanket over my head and a toe on the ground. To feel safer we left every light on in the living room and kitchen. At least we would see it easier when it flew around.

The sun couldn't come up soon enough. When morning finally arrived we felt drained and defeated. The three of us poked fun at each other, laughing about our reactions to him. We were skittish but still had to try to locate the bat. We all looked half halfheartedly, as none of us wanted to be the one to find it again.

"Unbelievable," Sharon said. "Look at that."

The bat had made its home next to the bright light bulb over the stairs. I looked up and shook my head. He had spent the entire night there, all quiet and content.

## FLYING UNWELCOME GUESTS

Good thing we left the light on for him. I guess it's not true that bats only like the dark.

Once we calmed down and took a deep breath again we called for help from Tom, a friend from down the road. He walked in with his big fishing net and worn tennis racquet, scooped it up and with one toss threw the bat outside. Back at the bat's home I am sure he had a good laugh about the wild night he had at the old cedar cottage when he scared the three women. Throughout the day, if we made direct eye contact we would laugh and remember how we acted like fools over a little bat. But truthfully we would probably act the same way again.

After that incident I decided to learn as much as I could about bats to try to understand them so I wouldn't be so afraid of such a little animal. I learned that bats are much more common over water because they are very dehydrated and also eat the bugs living near the water. The bat population has greatly increased over the years at Conesus Lake and once they have been in your house they leave a special marking so other bats know it is a good place to go. So I could imagine nights when the house was sealed up the bats would try to find any small hole or open window to get into. They would come in behind you when you walked in the door, and hid under the towels hung up on the clothesline. I began to develop bat phobia. I was constantly listening for them and I couldn't go to sleep without thinking about them.

Weeks later while I slept I heard a clip clip and I looked

## SOLD AS IS

up to see something black flutter past. In denial I hoped it was just a pretty blue bird. Once again I was in a battle, me against the critters. I grabbed my comforter from the bed and slinked downstairs like a worm. The multitude of bats were upstairs, I reminded myself. As I lay downstairs on the living room couch, I practiced my deep breathing and repeated mantras like, "They won't hurt me. Mr. Bat is more afraid of me than I am of him. They won't bite. They won't kill me." My positive self-talk usually helps, but not now. The whole time I wondered what the rabies shots would be like.

While I put my sheet over my head, seconds later, I felt a twitch of a wing brush by my head. It was no bird. I know my blood pressure must have spiked. One of the menacing bats ruffled my hair as it dive bombed me, and then swooped down to the ground. No fight in me, this was not going to be all out war tonight. I retreated to my car like a coward.

"All right, have your laughs," I said to the bats. I was finally in peace as I relaxed and fell asleep. I knew the bats couldn't get to me, at least for now. While I slept in the jeep, wrapped up in my blankets, fear overwhelmed me in my dream. I woke up in a startle, realizing that the car windows were left open all night. I envisioned an aerial attack and instinctively put my hand up to cover my face. I fumbled and attempted to roll up the windows. My car looked just like a cozy dark cave for the bats, but luckily none came in.

## FLYING UNWELCOME GUESTS

Hours before the sun had risen I reached for my cell phone. I had bat man's number on speed dial, and while leaving another message I struggled to keep my voice from cracking. I had a difficult time and did not want to break down and cry. After work I hurried home and listened to my voicemail, hoping to hear from the bat man. He had called in the morning and said he would stop by that afternoon or early evening.

He knew my house well and had gotten frustrated that we couldn't solve the bat problem. He brought his yellow fiberglass ladder and crawled around my roof and chimney, sealing every nook and cranny. When he finished we talked in the driveway for another few minutes before he hopped into his old truck.

"You are sealed up tight," he said in a reassuring voice. "There is no way any bat can get in here."

Sure enough, a few days later another sinister bat was flying around my living room again. In desperation, I called again. He said it must have been sleeping inside when he sealed up all the holes. It probably tried to fly around to get out and couldn't, he said.

"Okay," I said to him, "Now what do I do?"

With a straightforward tone he said, "Sit on your porch 'til it gets dark and pour yourself a stiff drink. Don't have any lights on in your house or porch and wait 'til you see it fly around the living room. Then let it out the sliding glass door."

"Really?" I said. Unfortunately he was serious.

## SOLD AS IS

I gave myself a shot of courage, also called gin and tonic, and reassured myself that I could do this. It was just a tiny black creature, after all. As I sat on the dark porch with a small blanket, and flashlight, my neighbor Matt asked what I could possibly be doing.

"I have to wait 'til it gets dark so I can flush the bat out."

He laughed and said, "Come on over and watch TV and I will help you."

What a deal. I had not watched TV since we cut down a tree and broke my cable line in May. I couldn't resist the extra help. So much for being independent. We watched the summer Olympics, and then at about 9 p.m. when it was dark we walked back into my house together. We came prepared for battle: flashlights, tennis racquets, fishing net and a hood over my head. You could have called me Velcro the way I stuck to Matt for fear of the black flutter monster.

In the almost pitch dark of the house we carefully made our way upstairs. We stood in silence and waited to hear the flap of the wings, and waited and waited. A couple of minutes passed and we finally went back and watched more TV. Just before 11 p.m. we repeated the bat hunt, returning to a silent house. No flap or flutter. I hoped the bat somehow was gone and it would be over. I slept on the couch for about an hour then I felt my stomach sink. I heard a flutter. I could feel my adrenaline as I crawled to the sliding glass door. I opened the door and the bat flew outside, just as it was planned four hours earlier.

## FLYING UNWELCOME GUESTS

I was exhausted and emotionally drained and slept once again with a sheet over my head and one eye open. It took me months to get over the fear of bats, to feel comfortable sleeping at night and not hear any phantom fluttering.

That was the last time I saw a bat, but the bat man had also discovered other unwelcome tenants.

When he was on the ladder patching up the holes on the roof he said, "Have you noticed a banging on your house? Drilling like sounds?"

I had, but didn't know what it was. Genuinely sympathetic, he said that woodpeckers had been pecking at the overhang by the roof. As I looked up I could see a row of small holes just like a power drill would make. It was left there by the Pileated woodpecker as he foraged for food.

"Termites or carpenter ants," he said.

"Thanks" I said as I thought that "Sold As Is" once again came in handy for my parents. Unfortunately for me, this would not be the end of my battles with pests.

# Revenge of the Bees

Spraying for the invading bees and waiting
for the mayhem to start.

*"Aerodynamically the bumblebee shouldn't be able to fly, but the bumblebee doesn't know it so it goes on flying anyway."*

Mary Kay Ash—Founder of Mary Kay, Inc.

The bats were the beginning of the war in critters that were trying to invade the cottage.

"Oh my, look at that." I said to my brother Glenn, pointing up to a large hornets' nest along the field stone

## SOLD AS IS

path next to the cottage. The hive was cemented to the board under the roof overhang, a gray tornado-shaped funnel larger than a basketball. It had a papery texture and at the lower half a hole about two inches in diameter where the black and white Bald-faced hornets would fly in and out just like central station. I kept daily tabs as the hive's girth widened abnormally fast, reminding me of Jack and the Beanstalk.

Glenn wanted to remove the nest in the cool of the day but I was apprehensive. We armed ourselves with two cans of long-distance bug spray and aimed to annihilate anything that flew, but were ready to fire at a moment's notice if they swarmed out. I was tired of the bats that had invaded my house, and this time I was determined to prevent the hornets from invading.

He climbed up a step ladder and edged close, then with a steady hand aimed for the target about three feet away. It was a tense moment as the powerful spray was directed to the small opening. I stumbled back and cowered behind the maple tree while I waited for the pandemonium to begin. I had a false sense of security—the tree wouldn't protect me. The hornets looked mean and were extremely quick-moving as the multitude escaped then spiraled into the ground. We watched for a few minutes as the activity in the hive slowed down and stopped. Finally, my brother took a canoe paddle and knocked the hive to the ground. I felt jubilant and empowered that we had won the battle of the hornets. The last thing I wanted was to be stung by

# REVENGE OF THE BEES

one of those ugly, long-legged things.

∽∾

It was mid-afternoon later that day. I lounged on the couch as I flicked on the TV, then noticed that the sliding glass door was open just a crack. My eye caught the sight of a tiny black object that flew full speed through the open door. It was a tiny honey bee on a mission, like it was given special orders from a high ranking commander bee to attack. I was too slow to react as both of my eyes followed the little buzz to his target, my left cheek. Befuddled and off balance I tumbled and thrashed on the floor. I slapped fiercely at my face, then my head and all over my chest as I tried to kill the little soldier. Once the commotion died down, I scoured the floor but found no evidence of the bee attack except for the black stinger thrust into my face. I was perplexed and dazed about what had just happened. Normally honey bees would slowly fly around food or flowers and not bother anyone. With a flick and shoo of the hand they would fly away unharmed.

Then I had an epiphany. We sprayed the large hornets' nest a couple of hours earlier and the hornets must have secreted an alarm pheromone to alert other bees in the area that they were in danger. I knew that bees could easily detect pheromones from their antenna and that the scent was very hard to wash off. I laid down to rest after all the excitement and my face began to swell. I squinted into the mirror as I made a valiant effort to pluck out the stinger.

## SOLD AS IS

I had some satisfaction once it was out but it was still red and puffy and I felt nauseous.

The next day I walked around the cottage with heightened awareness. Tenderly I moved the lawnmower and before I could react another little black bee stung me between my thumb and forefinger. I cussed as I slapped my hand and thrashed arms around on the ground. I retreated inside the cottage like there was an invisible creature chasing me. Still in disbelief, I started to soak my hand in ice.

Another two wonderful sunny summer days passed. I babysat my friend Max and socialized with friends from out of state. It was a recipe for an awesome day.

"Let's go out in the kayaks," my friend Laurie yelled.

I thought it was a fantastic idea. I grabbed the paddles along with the life jackets and my friends ran to pick out their favorite colored boat. As I started to delegate and organize the crew, I flipped over my canary yellow kayak and found there was a little black and yellow hornet waiting. My face was again the target and he stung me directly between my eyes. I screamed and ran, instinctively slapping my forehead with my hands. The hornet fell to the ground. My head throbbed and ached and was by far the most painful sting I had experienced.

This was the third time in a week I was stung yet they didn't bother any of the other visitors to the cottage. I was still on the bee "hit list." It was like I had tiny flying land

## REVENGE OF THE BEES

mines all around me and I had to be careful to look where I stepped or what I touched.

I wanted to be a good sport and try to ignore the latest incident, but it was not that easy. Throughout the day the puffiness in my face intensified along with the pain. It got to the point a few hours later that my eye swelled shut and I was concerned about scaring the little children. I was still watching Max, and together we drove to the emergency room where they provided me with an antihistamine and anti-inflammatory medicine to counteract the effects of the bee sting.

Once we got back to the cottage we flopped down on the couch. Despite all my drama, Max insisted on watching the animated cartoon called "Bee Movie". I cringed and weakly protested, but with my eye swollen shut I couldn't watch anyway. I was groggy and quickly fell asleep as he sat next to me and watched the movie about one of my least favorite creatures. It took two full days for my face to deflate back to normal.

In my battle the bees, they definitely prevailed. We had vanquished the rapidly growing hornets nest, but their friends heard their distress call and enacted vengeance on me.

# Lake Lore:
# Explosion on the 3rd of July

Frahnk, Frahnk. I was roused from a deep sleep one summer morning by the loud hoarse croaks that came from the lake. Rolling out of bed, reaching the silver handle to open the French doors, I saw the mist slowly rising off the still water. A beautiful bluish gray heron stood at the end of the dock with an impressive 6 foot wingspan, long s-shaped neck and narrow orange bill. His bellowing call was my alarm clock. Sensing danger from distant boat noises, he majestically tucked his neck toward his body and took off with a slow flap of his strong wings. What a wonderful way to start the day, I thought.

The circle of fire was one of the most special days of the year, the 3rd of July, when the lake owners strategically place approximately 10,000 road flares around the rim of the lake and all light them exactly at 10 p.m.

## SOLD AS IS

Parties began early and kids bubbled with excitement. As the sun went down more than 40 people gathered at my cottage for the celebration. It is a special night of snuggling up in blankets, toasting marshmallows while watching the children as they run around jazzed up on life and sugar.

A little dampness settled in the air, the snapping campfire was lit. The spectators pulled up, sitting on logs and folding chairs, mesmerized by the dancing of the red and orange flames. When the wind blew in their direction the warmed visitors tried to avoid the smoke. The little kids stood in a circle as the sparklers were lit. Poof, they came to life, brilliant white and red, whizzing around in a circle then fading in less than a minute. In the kitchen the white countertops were filled with food and snacks, overflowing colors of red white and blue napkins, cups and plates. Crockpot scents of barbecue, pulled pork and chili filled the air.

I heard a high pitched whistle that came from the end of the dock. There was a group of four or five teenagers anticipating blowing off firecrackers. They wanted a lighter. I was nervous—working in a hospital you hear all the horror stories about missing fingers and accidents from fireworks.

Up on the porch sitting at a glass round table my brother Barry and friends were playing a serious game of cards, looking professional and loaded with delicious snacks. Inside the cottage, my niece Erin and her two-year

## EXPLOSION ON THE 3RD OF JULY

old daughter Emma and four-year-old Taryn sat on the blue couch playing with Barbie dolls and watching "My Little Pony" on television. My nephew Tucker and Bob, who is a fireman, were in the kitchen making a pitcher of lemonade.

A firework called the "rocket" was the diameter of an adult's arm and positioned at the end of the dock. But after the fuse was lit, it accidentally tipped over backward. Instead of its intended course over the lake it headed straight into the numerous visitors sitting on the lawn. We gasped in horror and screamed as the flash of light passed next to our heads. We instinctively jumped out of the path of the screeching rocket as it flew straight into the crowd.

Somehow it missed everyone. Just seconds before, Barry had risen to walk away from the table. Erin went upstairs to put the baby down to sleep. It shattered the porch window, then BAM! A huge explosion, flash of red and white light and thick black gray smoke billowed from the living room. The rocket crashed through the living room window into the kitchen. Bob saw the flash and fell back as he grabbed Tuckers arm flinging him out of the rockets path. It bounced off the wall, changed direction and landed on the blue couch, starting a fire.

I was in shock. I couldn't run inside, so I just sat there. I knew the cottage was on fire and would burn down in a hurry if we didn't get inside quickly. The window was blown out, and through shattered glass and the smoke I

## SOLD AS IS

couldn't see the living room. In the shock of the blast, chaos and confusion, Erin upstairs thought a bomb went off. She wrapped her baby and ran outside to see fear and horror on faces of family and friends. People ran inside and together grabbed the couch and threw it out before the cottage caught on fire. The neighbors heard the commotion and came running, scared something tragic had happened. We are generally calm neighbors not used to causing such an upheaval.

All the group could talk about the rest of the night was the flying rocket. It was almost impossible that it flew right through a crowd of 40 people, smashed through the house and not one person was hurt. I know some higher power was looking out for us that night. In the aftermath of the incident we agreed as a family that we would not blow off fireworks ourselves. It's a decision I agree with down to my soul, but the larger significance of the night was the attachment that I felt toward the cottage when I saw it slipping away so quickly. In light of my journey to restore the cottage I realized that my love for the building was profound and encompassing.

# Lake Lore: Mutiny on the Water July 2005

Some of the poorest decisions in life can end up creating the best stories. My story of Mutiny on the water was a journey filled with silent winds, turbulent skies and a rough sea that needed to be calmed.

With only an hour of daylight left, the fluffy clouds that earlier looked liked rain now had blown away. My mid-summer excitement was heightened with the company of three friends who looked forward to a carefree boat ride around the shoreline—and one who wasn't so sure. My friend Debbie previously lived on Conesus Lake and had a fondness for the water. Janice lived in Niagara Falls and craved the excitement of WaveRunner rides and swimming. Susan was petrified of being in the water.

## SOLD AS IS

The only way she could enjoy it was from 50 yards away. Susan initially didn't want to come on the boat, but Janice coaxed and enticed her, eventually getting her to agree half-heartedly.

We planned a trip to the local restaurant where we would eat hors d'oeuvres and listen to tropical music. The porch door slammed as we dashed barefoot outside, tossing our flip flops onto the floor of the ski boat along with the life jackets, sweatshirts and towels. We waved goodbye to a few friends who stayed back and planned to join them after dinner for a campfire of marshmallows and s'mores.

The family boat was a 16-foot maroon and white Meracruiser speed boat. Debbie stood on the dock and cranked the large wheel around on the boat hoist which lowered the boat into the water with a gentle splash. While I held the boat close to the dock, they gingerly boarded and out-maneuvered each other for their favorite seat. I headed to the captain's chair and started up the motor. Seconds later I heard loud gasps.

"It's sparking!" Debbie yelped. "The motor is sparking. Shut it off."

I looked over my shoulder and noticed a flash and cluster of white sparks as I heard a crackle and popping sound. Two electrical wires connected to the motor had frayed and were exposed, creating sparks as they rubbed on each other. I didn't want this little problem to stop us so I wrapped black electrical tape around the wires to

# MUTINY ON THE WATER

prevent the occurrence again. Susan was now a little more skittish but Janice and I reassured her that the boat ride would be safe.

As we pulled away from the dock we entered into a classic summer evening on the lake. The sun glistened on the water, accentuating the little ripples created by the breeze. We buzzed along, swaying from rhythmic waves that slapped against the hull. Above us the sea gulls flew unorganized, searching for food as they squawked and chattered. We heard the distant throb of an engine and saw a teenage wake boarder performing aerial stunts. We watched and cheered him on in awe when he flipped around in a complete circle.

The orange twilight finally faded and was engulfed by the black sky. Celestial navigation was always a challenge, but I had done it before and knew the landmarks well. By law we needed to turn on the boat lights around sundown but as the darkness approached they would not light up. We motored on toward our destination and soon arrived at the docks of the restaurant. Debbie, Susan and Janice went to get food while I recruited a fellow boater to help repair our navigational lights. Lake people generally assist each other in times of need, so I was pleased when I found Ben, a robust 24-year-old who sat aboard a sailboat moored at the dock. He looked up and threw a wide smile as I approached him.

"Is this a great night or what?" he said. In a soft voice I asked if he could help fix the boat lights.

## SOLD AS IS

"Sure, I would be happy to help," he said eagerly.

He brought his small tool case to the unlit boat and with a screwdriver pulled out the burned light bulbs. As he worked we talked about how fortunate we were to be able to enjoy the lake and before I knew it the white lights lit up brightly again. The boat was now in tip top shape, no more sparks and we were legal with boat lights that shined brightly.

There is a well-attested superstition that says bad things come in threes. If I had been superstitious at this point I might have been worried that the third bad thing was yet to occur, but the thought never entered my mind.

At about 9 p.m. we walked lightly on the dock to return to the boat. We were surprised that it was still warm, a rare muggy night with temperatures that hovered around 80 degrees. On the ride back we felt free but isolated. There was not another boat in view and it was nearly five miles back to our shore. Minutes later I heard the motor misfire once followed by a slight sputter. I felt a twinge in my stomach, knowing intuitively that something wasn't right. I squinted my eyes and peeked down at the gas tank to see the arrow pointing to empty. I had added gas the previous day but in our excitement to get out to the boat I misjudged how much was left. I didn't have the heart to come clean and fought to maintain my composure. I looked straight ahead and scanned the shore while I did some mental arithmetic to figure out how long it would take for the motor to seize.

## MUTINY ON THE WATER

"Hey Ellen," Debbie said her hazel eyes lightening up.

"Let's see the beautiful red and blue lights that come from Mr. Stapletons' mansion on the west side of the lake. The colors fade in and out just like we had seen at South Beach."

"How about we head for the east shore," I whispered back as I leaned toward her. "We are on fumes."

She didn't respond, but we made eye contact and smiled. I pushed the throttle forward, wanting to get as far as we could before we stalled. About two minutes later I couldn't hide it anymore. There was a loud gurgle, sputter, and a couple of lunges and then the propeller stopped. The momentum kept us gliding briefly until we came to a stop in an uncomfortable silence. One by one each friend looked at me in disbelief. Initially Janice and Susan thought it was a prank, but it was no joke. We were out of gas and all alone in the middle of the lake.

"It cannot be true," Susan said shaking her head. The tone in her voice reflected her expression.

It was only a small lake, but to Susan it might as well have been the middle of the ocean. She assumed we would have to jump into the abyss and try to swim back to shore, more likely ending up at the bottom of the lake. Debbie and Janice were not as worried as they calmly started to discuss our options.

Minutes past as we were adrift. The cottage was still at least four miles away with nothing but darkness separating us. Debbie suggested we start to paddle so I felt around

## SOLD AS IS

on my hands and knees for the ash paddle, attempting to adjust my eyes to the dismal light. It would be a rudimentary way to travel in a motorboat but we had no other means to get back on our own. I rose slowly and gripped the wooden paddle in my hands as I perched on the front of the boat. As I plunged the paddle down we began to creep forward.

"I will not just sit here while you paddle back to shore," Susan exclaimed. "It is too long of a distance. How long will it take us? All night?"

"We can take turns paddling," I said to her. "It is only a few miles so it shouldn't take us more than a couple of hours."

I could sense that Susan deeply regretted agreeing to come. She stared straight ahead and made an effort as if to sit down, but stayed absolutely stiff and shifted from one foot to another while she kept a death grip on the vinyl seat.

I paddled to a steady rhythm—stroke, re-chamber, stroke. Every third stroke I tried to breath in my nose then out my mouth. I knew oxygen would increase my strength. Janice and Debbie each took turns paddling but tired quickly. With four people in the boat it was like we were pulling a heavy anchor. I tried to follow landmarks as we crept along, but I tired from being the human motor and took a break. I looked back and noticed that Susan had leaned over her purse and was scrambling in attempt to find her cell phone.

## MUTINY ON THE WATER

"What are you going to do?" I asked.

"To call 911 and get the Coast Guard to rescue us," she replied with fear in her voice. I laid down the paddle, wanting to elaborate calmly to help her understand.

"They won't come. There is no Coast Guard on the lake now and the sheriff left hours ago. Besides, we don't need the Coast Guard or the police. All we have to do is paddle."

"Ellen do you have to stop the paddle and set it down every time you argue with Susan?" Debbie said. "Don't turn around to talk, just paddle."

Debbie was right, every time I tried to calm Susan I stopped the paddle along with the boat.

"I can't do this anymore," Susan snapped back at Debbie. "I have to call Robert back at the cottage. He will rescue us."

"Robert couldn't rescue us if he wanted to because we have the only motorboat," I told her. "He would have no way to tow us back and can't use the WaveRunner at night."

Janice leaned over and snatched the cell phone from Susan's purse. Susan made repeated attempts to grab the phone back from Janice, who pleaded with her to stay calm.

In front, I tried to focus on paddling. My strikes had to be deep and strong to move the bulky boat. Occasionally I looked back out of the shadows to keep track of the mayhem, but when Janice saw this she tried to motivate me to

## SOLD AS IS

paddle again. Susan frowned as she sat in silence, trying to suppress her fear. Janice and Debbie sequestered her to the back of the boat and reassured her that everything would okay.

As I paddled I thought about the irony of the three of us, close in so many ways but varying so greatly on how to approach our nocturnal situation. I thought, "Let the adventure begin." We were safe, it was warm and the lights now worked. To me, this was nothing more than a little inconvenience. Janice, herself a veteran of a few cottage mishaps, had been excited and enjoyed a little adventure. This was the kind of experience she would remember with fondness. For Debbie, who enjoyed the calm tranquility of the rippled water and the humid weather, it was a peaceful experience, a chance to connect with nature. But for Susan, who doesn't enjoy being in or on the water, her mind swam in a sea of uncertainty. As we inched upstream in uncharted waters she was on a quest for answers.

∽∾

Back at shore the cottage lights were brilliantly lit and the yellow embers of the campfire drifted up with the gentle breeze as the pine wood snapped and cracked. Our friends lounged around the campfire in Adirondack chairs, the flames intensifying their faces. They enjoyed the conversation and soaked up the gossip of current events, unaware of our predicament out in the darkness.

As the muffled sounds of voices drifted across the

## MUTINY ON THE WATER

smooth black water, the voices around the campfire lowered and ears strained to decipher the sounds. They were perplexed about what could possibly be making so much noise in the lake during the dead of night.

"I am not going to do that," they heard someone say in a firm tone. "I cannot paddle anymore, quit bugging me."

Other voices competed with the chatter until someone around the fire said, "Quiet, let's hear this." Robert rose from his chair and moved closer to the water's edge, his neck craning toward the commotion in an attempt to amplify the sound.

"No you will not call them for help."

"Listen to that," Robert said. All the heads were now turned toward the familiar voices that came from the water.

Our voices grew closer and louder and soon it became apparent to them that the calamity on the lake came from the four friends who departed hours earlier. We couldn't hear from the boat but on shore they erupted in laughter. Our friend James walked away from the fire and extinguished every light in the cottage, hoping the stranded crew wouldn't be able to locate the dock or the cottage.

Twenty minutes later the boat paddled back to the hoist where it began and the four of us quickly made an agreement not to tell anyone of the experience. This pact would only last two minutes. As we walked down the dock toward the shore we acted like nothing unusual had occurred, but the moment they saw us our campfire friends burst out laughing and pantomimed our arguments on the

## SOLD AS IS

water. They were proud of themselves and admitted that they turned off all the cottage lights.

Even after being stranded together we are still very good friends and laugh about the situation. Susan ran off the dock that night never to board our boat again, even during the daylight. Debbie and I smile whenever the tale is retold, while Janice remembers the excitement and looks forward to another cottage mishap.

This story has become a campfire favorite on warm summer nights. If they stretch their heads out toward the dark, those who hear the tale can almost hear the cries from the stranded sailors.

# The Keys to my Success

During the renovations to help me focus on my goals I journaled daily, read inspirational quotes and created a dream board of pictures depicting my abounding success. My visualizations were simular to a mental video revealing pictures of my completed dream.

Studies have shown that the subconscious mind controls 83 percent of our thoughts while our conscious mind controls only 17 percent. The reticular activating system is a part of the brain that connects the outside world stimulus to our inner thoughts and emotions. It filters out things that are not important and alerts us to pay attention to items that are relevant. If my thoughts contained an emphasis on success then my subconscious would latch onto the things that would create or attract more prosperity. As my predominant thoughts and feelings matched, situations attracted people and things to

## SOLD AS IS

fulfill my goals. Those times during my renovation when everything fell into place and the frequency was just right were almost magical.

⁓⚬⚭

The new pontoon boat my father bought in 2008 was scheduled to be delivered by the end of the week, but to make room we would have to sell the old boat hoist. It was a tall order because three mature maple trees had been cut down near the shore and blocked access to the old hoist. I hired my nephew Bobby a dairy farmer, to split the logs and clear away the pile of intertwined branches, but the weather was unfavorable for cutting wood on the weekends. Then, when planting season arrived the trees came second to planting corn. The professional tree service was booked up for at least two weeks so I was left to attempt it on my own.

The pile of wood started at the water line and stretched back at least 30 feet. I felt unsettled as I slowly chipped and trimmed away small branches with a hand saw. But as hard as I worked I could do little against the mountain of trees I had to conquer. Before long I retreated back to the porch and cupped my head in my hands, visualizing that the fallen trees were gone. I stopped thinking of myself as a victim and shifted my thoughts to optimism and empowerment. Three times a day I would meditate about achieving my smooth lawn free of debris. I didn't know how it would happen but had faith it would all fall into place.

## THE KEYS TO MY SUCCESS

I advertised the hoist for sale on the computer and received a phone call within the hour. The potential buyer, Samuel, looked at the hoist and wanted to buy it but the fallen trees blocked his access. He said in a light voice he was a lumberjack and his chainsaw was in his van, already gassed up.

My creative mind kicked into high gear. I asked if he would be willing to cut a pathway to the hoist in exchange for the wood. He pulled out his chainsaw and started cutting. One by one he sliced through the logs and rolled them out of the way. When he was done he gestured for me to come over to the hoist, where he pointed to the brown rust stains on the pipes. My confidence plummeted. The weak areas were not safe for a boat and would have to be welded. I was devastated, but then looked up to see Samuel smiling.

"I have to dismantle the hoist to relocate it to my boat," he said. "When I get back home I will just weld it back together. I own a metal shop, so it won't be any trouble at all."

It was quite amazing odds to sell the hoist the same day I advertised it to a lumberjack who also cut up the logs and just happened to own a metal shop. I sat down to absorb the implications of what happened and my wonderful stroke of luck.

With the high cost of materials and contractors in

## SOLD AS IS

such a lengthy, major renovation project, money was always a concern. I did however come from a place of abundance, not from a place of scarcity. I was going to focus my thoughts on wealth and knew when I focused on what I desired would fall into place. For every financial obstacle that arose a solution always seemed to materialize.

I owned an 18-foot Chrysler Buccaneer sailboat that I advertised for sale to help pay for renovations. I received a call from Lee, who said he wanted to refurbish a sailboat but was short on funds. He asked if we could negotiate on the price. I felt a spark of creativity when he said he was a contractor, and I asked if he would be willing to do some work in exchange for the boat. We were both elated. He could now live out his dream and with his help I would be closer to mine.

The kitchen floor was rough plywood but I wanted finished hardwood. The porch floor boards were soft and starting to rot from the rainwater dripping from the roof. He agreed to install new floors for the kitchen and put in new gutters in exchange for the sailboat, motor and trailer.

For a month he stopped by on the weekends and chipped away at the projects. I stayed with him as he worked, holding the ladder while we discussed our love of sailing. When the projects were completed and he pulled away with the boat in his trailer, I knew his passion would make him successful in completing the boat's transformation.

## THE KEYS TO MY SUCCESS

About a month later, while out on my WaveRunner I spotted a familiar white sail with a black pirate sword. It was my boat, all refurbished and on its maiden voyage. I waved hello with a smile on my face and kindness in my heart.

The way the cottage looked in June of 1996 before my dream became a reality.

In July 2009 porch railings were installed, thirty trees were cut down and rain gutters were hung.

## SOLD AS IS

The projects of August 2010 included replacing the porch floor, posts and reinforcing the porch roof.

August 2010 brought a new deck above the porch.

It was January 2009. After a summer and fall of renovations the kitchen, storage room and bathroom were completed and the furnace was installed. I was ready to

## THE KEYS TO MY SUCCESS

continue my momentum of construction and begin to renovate the living room. The walls had open studs and needed new electrical wiring, insulation and drywall. The floors and ceiling had to be strengthened with the addition of five new windows.

My desire was to find a trustworthy carpenter who would work two or three days a week and charge no more than $20 an hour. Weeks later I was sitting in the cafeteria at work and enjoying a cup of green tea when I noticed an old friend who had moved away to the Thousand Islands. Marion and her husband John were very down-to-earth and genuinely kind. She said they were going to move back over the winter for three months. Then it hit me like a bolt of lightning—her husband was a retired finished carpenter with 50 years of experience. He was the answer I was seeking and it just walked up to me.

The next week we met at the cottage and developed a construction strategy. It was so cold and the wind was whistling straight off the frozen lake right into the living room. My feet were numb, my teeth chattering. We drove to a local restaurant to thaw out and I felt excited but impatient. John reviewed his plan and told me he could work two or three days a week and would go slow, taking the whole winter. When I asked his hourly rate he said, "How about $20 an hour?"

We would start in a couple of weeks, but first I had to get a heating source. I found a close friend who could lend me a kerosene heater for three months. When it was fired

## SOLD AS IS

up it loudly rumbled and rattled and the heat poured out. I wrapped the living room in plastic to try and hold in some of the heat. It was a small slice of heaven in a frigid house. We were never warm but it made the cold bearable. The neighbors invited us over for bathroom breaks and warm drinks. When the cold became unbearable we stopped for weeks at a time and hoped for a warm up.

Marion and I were John's assistants, but we ended up more like Ethel and Lucy. It was always a comedy of errors, like cutting the boards the wrong way but acting as though we were experts. John completed the living room wiring, insulation, dry wall and strengthened the ceiling. I walked in one day and became misty eyed as I saw the beautiful fireplace hearth he created, just like I had pictured. He installed four windows and one octagon window. After John installed the octagon window, I would catch myself staring out in wonder. Outsiders must have thought there was a TV screen there.

When I met John the carpenter, the attraction was immediate and my decision automatic. It was the same with Samuel the lumberjack and David the contractor. I focused on financial abundance and screened out my intrusive thoughts of financial inadequacies. I saved thousands of dollars scouring all kinds of places to buy building materials—discontinued kitchen cabinets, countertops, shower and vanity. The answers came from contractors, hardware

## THE KEYS TO MY SUCCESS

stores, scratch and dent sales and word of mouth. I surrounded myself with positive successful people who walked with me down my path to success, a fine tuned harmony of people who provided me incredible strength. It flowed over from my neighbors, friends and family who watched my progress, shared opinions and supported my goals as the transformation grew daily.

In January 2009, the bitter cold living room renovation began.

Ellen painting the new octagon window.

New windows were installed along with ductwork and electrical wiring. Insulation was placed in the floors, walls and then covered in drywall.

John the carpenter designed new doors under stairway

A walkway was cut through living room wall and
the dark wainscoting was painted light green.

In June 2010 a railing by the stairs was built.
The bathroom and fireplace tile floors were completed.

# Healing Waters

---

*"For every step in life, live it fully without any regrets, and create many memories along the way."*

Michael R. Steger — Poet

Year after year the cottage was the one thing in my life that was stable. In April of my sophomore year in high school my family moved to a larger farm far away from where we lived my whole life. My brother and I stayed to finish the school year living with my grandmother who remained on the family farm and did not want to move. My high school was new along with the town, but the cottage was the same. It was old and weathered the rock in my life. When my heart was ripped open, it was a place to heal, contemplate life and accept its unfairness.

## SOLD AS IS

I was introduced to Rick Lewis in 1996. I was meeting friends at the marina where Rick moored his motorboat on Lake Ontario. It was a day with impending rain clouds and the lake had high wave warnings, so we stayed on shore and talked about adventure. I was captivated by his stories of pirates and sailing around the Caribbean while visiting friends on St. John's. He loved jokes, sailboats, was full of opinions and yet a free spirit. We shared a love of tropical locations. He owned a floral shop and I had a degree in horticulture. Within a few months we went into business together, installing and maintaining tropical plants for businesses and restaurants.

Rick was magnetic, his dark red hair and intense smile drawing people in. Friends and family would gravitate to his generous heart. He was a special education teacher, business owner and landscaper. He had divorced many years earlier with no children. Average in stature but with a very tall personality, he was vibrant at 45. Rick admired my spirit and encouraged me to always be a better person, to live life to the fullest. He was my business partner and best friend.

In March 1999 I noticed the normally energetic Rick had been lethargic for weeks. He knew something was wrong. He went to the hospital where he completed numerous tests and spoke to physicians. When we spoke he downplayed how serious it was and how unhealthy he felt, but inside I could tell he was scared. We would talk on the phone every day just to check in with each other, but he

## HEALING WATERS

didn't complain. On weekends our plans were all about being on the water, either on his 30-foot motorboat or at my cottage. Our philosophy was to enjoy life, summed up by the "Life is Good" t-shirts he wore.

A few weeks later on a cool spring night, we took the chill off while soaking in his hot tub outside. We listened to the crickets and talked about our summer plans. When we moved inside to his living room, the music was turned up and naturally we danced. Acting like kids, we laughed and listened to the sounds of Jimmy Buffet, wishing we were both in Margaritaville.

Minutes later, Rick's face turned a little flush. He flopped down on the couch and grabbed my arm gently pulled me over to him and pointed for me to sit down. He tried to smile but the distant tears in his eyes were stronger than he could bear.

"The doctors discovered I have colon cancer," he blurted out. "The prognosis is poor. They give me six months to live." He was then silent for a moment as he got choked up. After few seconds he looked over at me and said sadly, with a slight smile and a tilt of his head, "Do want to travel the world?"

I slouched down, my legs growing wobbly. I was now flush and tried to push down the tears. It took a few minutes for my mind to process his words as they repeated over and over in my head: "I have six months to live." How was this possible? I couldn't fathom the news. Weeks passed as I absorbed the realization of his situation. It

## SOLD AS IS

was easy to just stay in denial, as this can be a good-short term mechanism to help cope. Rick stayed focused on his plan to travel the world in three months. I was so proud of him, facing his diagnosis with dignity and strength. I wished I could stop my life to participate in his last journey, but his trip was too lengthy and I couldn't take that much time off from work. I would have to envision the world through his phone calls, pictures and postcards.

He set out to travel the world flying first class, exotic tropical destinations such as Tonga, Bora Bora, Tahiti, New Zealand, Australia and Hawaii. He would rent cabanas on the beach, charter sailboats and scuba dive. But most importantly, he went to forget about being sick. While he was on his world trip I tried to absorb and digest the reality of his situation.

⁂

One afternoon in late June, with the sun blazing and the water twinkling I was crossing Lake Ontario in a motorboat with three friends. We were returning from a four-day trip to Canada and were about 14 miles from shore. The wave conditions were fantastic and slight breeze was producing ripples and small waves.

I tugged and squeezed into my full length wet suit and snapped on my life vest, prepared myself for the 65 degree water and dived in head first. It quickly invigorated my spirit and cooled my body. My friend Billy was leaning over the side of the boat and threw me the slalom ski

## HEALING WATERS

which is a long single water ski with two bindings to hold both feet in place. I adjusted the binding and struggled to wiggle in my foot. Billy threw the ski rope toward me like a lasso and I grasped the ski line, circling my fingers around the handle. I leaned back, pulling my legs in toward my chest, keeping my arms straight as the boat inched forward to take in the slack. I made eye contact with Billy and yelled, "Hit it." My slalom ski crested the water and skimmed across like I was floating.

Loud cheers arose as I dipped down into the crevice of a deep wave. My adrenaline flowed. I jumped a big wave, catapulting me high in the air. I leaned back, carving the lone ski through the water as it sprayed eight feet of mist, and I weaved back and forth across the deep wake created by the boats dual motors.

I felt exhilarated but my enjoyment only lasted a few minutes. As I jumped across a deep wave I was pulled off balance. It happened very quickly. My body twisted as the ski stopped against the side of the tall wave. I had fallen dozens of times, but this one was very different. My momentum continued while the ski stayed motionless. I fell hard and struggled to regain my balance. I experienced excruciating pain in my left knee and instinctively reached down toward the sensation. To my horror I discovered that my kneecap was dislocated. I floated helplessly on my back, unable to swim or move. I was in shock. I screamed for help as Billy dived into the water and grabbed the back of my life jacket. He swam me back to the boat and the

## SOLD AS IS

others helped pull me aboard.

They tried to reassure me but I could tell from their faces this was a very serious injury. The leg swelled quickly and I was soon unable to move it at all. For the next two hours as we rode back to the shore I laid on the floor of the boat wincing at every bump and wave. Once at the harbor, my friends made a human chair by holding their arms under my legs. It was a challenge to try to get me in the car as I couldn't get my knee to bend at all. During the car ride to the hospital I was forced to lay on the floor sideways taking up the entire backseat.

The emergency room doctor give me some medicine for the pain then drained the fluid that had accumulated, gave me a knee brace and crutches. The initial diagnosis was a severe dislocation of the patella and a torn meniscus. In five days I was scheduled to have arthroscopic surgery to repair and clean up the tissue fragments. Not only did I hurt physically but it was painful for my inner spirit. It was not part of my nature to sit around inactive.

I had a second surgery a month later to stabilize the kneecap, helping the patella fit in the groove better. Waking up in the recovery room, the surgeon said I would have to plan on an even more extensive surgery in a few weeks to realign the leg. He called this surgery an osteotomy, where the leg bone is cut and realigned, held together with metal screws. The tendons would then be reattached to stabilize my kneecap in a new point on my shin bone. I would be laid up for eight weeks before I could go back to work and

## HEALING WATERS

even after the recovery my left knee would never be the same. I would lose the ability to kneel down, and would take the better part of year to be able to run.

"Be prepared for a life of chronic ache, stiffness and loss of sensation," my doctor warned.

To help cope I had to stay in denial while I slowly absorbed the prognosis. My doctor said I shouldn't risk being on a waterski again. This was very hard news because it was one of my favorite sports.

After the July 15 surgery I spent four days in the hospital. My leg boasted a 9-inch long, bright red scar and I had a brace the entire length of my leg. Even worse, I felt the true essence of who I was had gone. I needed to be active to feel alive and fulfilled, and with that in doubt I started to feel sorry for myself. It was difficult accepting my limitation. Daily I struggled with the crutches, and blamed my knee. It prevented me from participating in the activities I loved and in my mind it was no longer part of my healthy body. I became detached.

⁂

Rick was now back from his world trip, cut short by a month when he got sick and needed medical assistance to treat his cancer. He was weak and fatigued, but optimistic about his life, ready to live it with a vengeance. Rick and I sat on the beach and watched the water and the world pass by. We contemplated life and wondered what it would be like to not be part of this world. We stayed at

## SOLD AS IS

the cottage a great deal of the days talking about life and what it will be like to not be part of this world. We were particularly grateful for our loved ones who would come and go, bringing us food and encouragement. Rick would try to sugarcoat his situation when he noticed his friends became somber. He always had a stupid joke to lighten the mood.

We became confidantes, two wounded souls who would encourage each other. I would hobble along slow, awkwardly using my crutches to walk, but would steady him when he was emotionally and physically weak. We were however at opposite ends of the spectrum. I wished for time to speed up so my body would heal. Rick desperately wanted to stop time to live as long as possible.

Neither of us was accustomed to going slow. In our predicament of limited mobility, we had to shift our negative thoughts and channel our energy to find ways to be active again. We both craved the surge of adrenaline that came so frequently to us before.

Three weeks passed and I started to feel significantly better. I was stir crazy and itching to do more than just sit under the elm tree. Our antidote was to move into action. His treatment was to have a purpose in life, not just fight cancer. He decided he could do that by helping me heal.

We brainstormed and came up with a detailed plan on how I could ride the WaveRunner. I had to wrap my entire leg in plastic and seal it with duct tape. I slowly hobbled to the dock being careful not to fall in, swaying

# HEALING WATERS

like a penguin. Once I was far enough down the dock I threw my crutches, laid down on the wood and rolled on my side. Stretching and leaning over, I reached the handlebars then pulled myself ungracefully up on to the seat. Rick already had the machine warmed up and ready to go. Once we were on the lake our health issues disappeared. We buzzed and skimmed across the water, feeling the wind whip at our faces. Being out on the water our spirits drastically changed. Rick for a moment felt healthy and cancer-free. I was mobile and able to experience the excitement I craved. We spent hours on the water at times just stopping the motors as we drifted around and talked I wanted to drink up these moments.

Riding on the WaveRunner was fun, but Rick decided it was time for us to really live. He leased a red, expensive convertible Mitsubishi 3000GT for three years. He drove it with absolute determination and strength. We drove to many of the local restaurants around Rochester and had a goal of visiting every Finger Lake in the area. He was always generous and would order lobster and champagne.

He wanted to surround himself with comfort. He bought us matching deluxe lounge chairs and two WaveRunners. Back at the cottage, we turned up the stereo to dance the best we could, two wounded souls hobbling along to the beat.

Rick knew I wanted to learn to sail, so he decided he was going to teach me himself. He had always owned a boat of some kind and sailing was in his blood. It had

## SOLD AS IS

been six weeks, and now I could walk around slowly or hop without my crutches. I was ready. He bought me a 16-foot fast performance sailboat. It holds two people and performs best at a 45 degree angle, with one side up in the air and the sailor's body hanging over the water. One of my hands stayed on the rope controlling the sail, the other clutched the tiller to steer. It took great coordination to steer while only the balls of my feet were in contact with the side of the boat. I discovered quickly that the boat required precision movements or it could quickly turn upside down. We sailed daily, him barking out commands as I learned the intricacies of sailing.

"Pull on the main sail," he would shout with confidence. I would pull in the rope, push on the tiller and it would accelerate hard to the right.

"Stop it from luffing," he would say in a more frustrated tone. Luffing is a noise sails create when the wind isn't hitting at the correct angle. The loose sail will just flap back and forth, the boat at a standstill.

This was a metaphor for Rick's life. He wanted desperately to have the cancer luff, but over time the wind blew and it accelerated. Once the cancer spread and he was unable to fight fatigue, Rick lost significant weight and was confined to a wheelchair. The sad day finally came when he was unable to sail with me anymore. He could only sit in his lounge chair under the cottonwood tree near the dock.

I had told him I was afraid to sail alone. I had created in my mind new self doubt, questioning my skill level. Rick frowned and shook his head, his voice and mannerisms showing his annoyance with me. He took a deep breath, sighed and told me how we all have "active and inactive intentions." I sat down on the grass, eager and ready to soak up his knowledge.

He looked serious as he spoke. "Ellen, our brains are continuously exposed to multitudes of random thoughts, but we choose which ones to focus on and which ones to ignore. Every action we take stems from an intention that is either beneficial or detrimental. Inactive intentions are

## SOLD AS IS

negative, they impede our goals contributing to fear and can harm our well-being. They can overwhelm us and are focused not on fact, but unknown doubts or helplessness that we have created in our mind."

He took a deep breath and leaned forward.

"Active intentions are optimistic and are created from thoughts that benefit our ambitions or dreams. They can be aspiration, endurance or fortitude. When you can exclude ambivalence you have a clear vision."

He explained that my inactive intentions were sabotaging my thoughts about sailing alone. He reminded me I would be safe if I flipped or turtled the boat, that I had a strong grasp of basic seamanship. He had taught me how to shift my body weight to get the momentum up to bring

## HEALING WATERS

it back upright if the boat did a flip. My self-doubt was not based on fact but a bunch of "what if" scenarios like losing the wind and not being able to get back to shore or coming into shore too fast and not being able to stop.

Rick watched on from shore during my first solo mission. The lake was slightly rough, but I could feel each wave coming and anticipate it. The boat would oscillate, rise and fall. I grasped the tiller and pulled in the main sail, making it accelerate and tip sideways very quickly.

As I sailed my thoughts drifted back to the shore where he was sitting. Rick was slipping away and yet desperately wanted to throw me his rope to help me live a wiser life. I thought about what he said about success depended on focusing my intention. I knew that every action I took would have a consequence, it could enrich my life or surpress my creativity. As my life progressed I would try to focus on my active intentions and block the inactive ones.

As I approached the dock I quickly lowered the two sails and the boat slowed down. I jumped into the water and slid the front of the boat onto the boards of the boat hoist. As I cranked the wheel around in a circle and the boat was lifted up out of the water, I felt waves of gratitude flood my mind. The ride was a success. I did wonderfully.

Time was growing short for Rick. He was very tired and would sleep a lot. When he walked his head was low and his feet scuffed against the floor, but his smile and

## SOLD AS IS

hope always remained. One early evening in September Rick was in the bedroom facing the water where he had been asleep for more than 15 hours. Our friends had visited but no one wanted to go upstairs to check on him because they didn't want to see him in that condition.

I heard the floor creak and then creak again. He must have gotten out of bed. I slowly opened the bedroom door and peaked inside, where Rick stood leaning on the bed with one arm. His smile was almost aglow. He faced the French doors and looked through the small panes of glass cloudy with dust.

In a strained voice he whispered, "I dreamed I had died and gone to heaven and it was all filled with shiny gold. Then I woke up. I looked out and saw the sky was golden, reds and yellow all blended together. It was the most beautiful sunset I have ever seen."

Tears streamed down my face. I hugged Rick and helped him back down on the bed, where we laid facing each other. I wrapped my arms around him and didn't want to let him go. I wanted time to stop, I clung on to this moment. His breath was shallow and irregular. He looked like a skeleton of the vibrant person he once was.

When I came down my friends looked up at me from a distance. My tears did not stop. I shuffled to the porch and grabbed my underwater camera, carefully putting the strap over my neck. I walked sadly down to the beach where I took a magical picture of the sunset. It was even more beautiful now, deeper golden just like Rick's heaven.

# HEALING WATERS

To me the picture represents love, peace, reflection and the healing cottage.

A couple of days later I noticed eight missed voicemail messages and surmised that something had happened. Rick had passed away at home, surrounded by his family.

---

Four days after Rick passed away his family came to my cottage to repossess the sailboat, two WaveRunners, stereo and other things he had bought. Rick's intentions in leaving the boat for me were better than his follow through—-he never put it in my name. Because it was registered in his name it became the property of his estate. I felt devastated as they pulled away with my boat on the trailer. Rick's generosity was more than I could comprehend at the time. The family didn't understand why he had bought me a $5,000 boat. I overheard at his funeral that they had planned to sell it as soon as possible and already had an interested buyer. I was dismayed.

Summoning my active determination, I hired a lawyer to retrieve my boat. Rick had bragged to everyone who would listen that he bought it for me to teach me how to sail, so I asked them to put in writing their understanding that he had purchased the boat as a gift.

Three weeks passed after sending my request to the estate lawyers and I heard nothing. I learned from a mutual friend of Rick's brother that the lawyer had no intention of ever giving the boat back. They ripped away the dream Rick

## SOLD AS IS

had for me. My lawyer planned to take them to court, as we served his estate the court papers, my only recourse left.

The phone rang at 8 a.m. on December 23. It was Rick's brother.

"The estate cannot be settled with a potential lawsuit. I will deliver the boat back to the cottage early this afternoon," he said hastily.

I put the phone down and cried as a huge weight of emotion was released, but the ordeal was not over. On his way to the cottage the trailer received a flat tire, then a ticket for an unregistered vehicle. Rick's brother called and asked if I would pick it up at his house instead. My brother Glenn got his flatbed truck and together with my father we drove 100 miles to Rick's hometown. Hours later we pulled into his family driveway, and sitting there was Rick's car, WaveRunners and his canoe. It was sad but final. Our flatbed truck delivered the sailboat back home to the cottage where it belonged. I was choked up and misty eyed, and I missed him so much.

It was the day after christmas, almost four months after he passed away and I was having a night of restless sleep. I tossed around until finally toward morning I fell into a deep sleep. I experienced a colorful dream that was so vivid it seemed real. In the dream I lived back in the suburbs at my old house. I watched television in my living room while I ironed my lab coat for work.

## HEALING WATERS

Outside the large picture window snowflakes hung in the air, as if someone had shaken a snow globe. Out of nowhere, with no knock the door flew open and Rick was there. He leaned over and knocked the snow from his boots then smiled and walked in nonchalantly.

In shock, I raced up to him and hugged his healthy body. We sat down on the wooden chair and I stared at him.

"Rick, you passed away," I said with bewilderment. "What are you doing here?"

He calmly sat next to me and chuckled. I told him everything that happened since he left. Talking to him I was energized and couldn't wait to tell all our friends that it was just a horrible mistake and Rick was still here. I was euphoric.

When I told him everything that happened with the sailboat, he didn't react or look upset. Rick was not disappointed with his family. He took my hand and caressed it, and after a moment slowly looked up at me and smiled. With compassion and remorse he said, "I didn't have anything to give you for Christmas this year, so your gift from me was the sailboat." His voice lowered a notch, "I delivered our sailboat back for you, Ellen. You were meant to sail it."

I woke up teary eyed and somber. The dream seemed so real. I felt like he was still taking care of me from beyond just as he had on earth. I know there is a connection from death to the earth, and I feel Rick around whenever I hear "Margaritaville."

## SOLD AS IS

Just like Rick taught me that I could raise the sails to catch certain winds, I choose which thoughts to hold onto and which to let pass through. With slight movements my sails could change direction, catching gentle winds that propelled me to my destination or destructive winds that blew me off my path.

The cottage can't heal the body but it has a way of healing the wounded soul. The long scar on my knee no longer represents a painful accident or operations. I have learned to love my knee, even with its deficiencies. It now represents how critical it is to appreciate every single day. Because of the lesson on the shore that day I strive to always live my life with active intention, following my dreams without doubt or fear. His wisdom provided me with a deeper insight that guided me with fulfilment and gratitude.

His love of adventure continued to live on in my heart. I still have my sailboat proudly sitting in the boat hoist at the cottage, and I named it "Tropical Dreams" after Rick's desire to travel the world. I have traveled the world myself fulfilling my own dreams of adventure. As I visited some of my favorite places—Beirut, Jordan, Egypt, Syria, Honduras, Europe and Hawaii. I know he was there with me, guiding me safely along the way.

# What's Next

When I bought "Sold As Is" the to-do list was insurmountable. Once I began to complete the renovations and landscape I focused on what I had completed to keep the momentum going. My experience provided a time to reflect upon my life. I spent dozens of days painting and thinking about the future of the cottage and my reflections have enabled me to grow in areas that I would have never expected. Through perseverance I was able to forge through any blocks that appeared as I chipped away slowly and surrounded myself with people who shared my vision.

The future plans of the cottage include hooking up to a permanent water source, replacing both dormers and getting rid of the unwelcome guests of carpenter ants that attracted hungry wood peckers. The upstairs remains original, with open studs and wainscoting walls. It is dark

## SOLD AS IS

and weathered with scuff marks from over the generations. But it is comforting and holds tight the memories of the original cottage. As time passes the character of the upgraded cottage will unravel to create a new generation of memories as the history of the "Sold As Is" cottage continues to unfold around every turn and renovation mishap.

My ancestors were part of the lake and intertwined with the cottage in the same way I am. The next generation will have a cottage filled with memories and stories of adventure chronicled along the way. And because of the structural enhancements I made the strength of the cottage will endure along with the memories.